8.20 Russell & Russell 1.68 (Swearingen)

THE ALBIGENSIAN HERESY

VOLUMES I AND II

The Albigensian Heresy

VOL. I

BY THE REV.

H. J. WARNER. M.A.

Henry James

NEW YORK / RUSSELL & RUSSELL

THIS BOOK CONSISTS OF
VOLUME I, FIRST PUBLISHED IN 1922
VOLUME II, FIRST PUBLISHED IN 1928
PUBLISHED BY THE SOCIETY FOR PROMOTING
CHRISTIAN KNOWLEDGE
REISSUED, 1967, BY RUSSELL & RUSSELL
A DIVISION OF ATHENEUM HOUSE, INC.
L. C. CATALOG CARD NO: 66-27174
PRINTED IN THE UNITED STATES OF AMERICA

REPRINTED FROM A COPY IN THE COLLECTIONS OF
THE NEW YORK PUBLIC LIBRARY

22644

CONTENTS

CHAPTER I

CHAPTER II

CHAPTER III

CHAPTER IV

CHAPTER IV (*continued*)

CHAPTER V

INTRODUCTION

THE interest and importance of the so-called Albigensian Heresy* lie in the fact that while it bears "a local habitation and a name," its actual habitation was not local, and its name is misleading. Its origin must be traced back to pre-Christian Ages, and its fruits will remain for ages to come. Its current title is inexact and incomplete; *inexact*, because Albi was not the *fons et origo* of a movement which, although it took deepest root in Southern France, was sporadic throughout Central and Western Europe ; *incomplete*, because the movement was not one heresy, but many, defying rigid classification, heterogeneous, self-contradictory, yet united in opposition to the Church of Rome. It is a mere accident of history that the name is derived from Albi, for Albi was but one, and that by no means the most important town infected. The storm-centre was the great city of Toulouse, which Peter de Vaux-Sarnai describes as

* The word "heresy" ($al\rho\epsilon\sigma\iota s$) originally carried with it no censure, but rather approval. In classical Greek it means (1) "free choice" (abstract), (2) "that which is chosen," (3) "those who make the choice, a sect or school." In ecclesiastical Greek (LXX) it is used to render נְדָבָה, "a free-will offering" (Lev. xxii. passim) ; in the N.T. it means "an opinion," whether true, false or neutral, or "those who hold such opinions." The Pharisees (orthodox), the Sadducees (rationalist), the Christians (schismatic) are alike described as "heresy," where perhaps "school" or "party" would be the more modern rendering (Acts v. 17, xv. 5, xxiv. 5, 14, xxvi. 5, xxviii. 22). St. Paul's use wavers between an opinion which is the outcome of legitimate freedom of thought, and positive schism. (Cf. 1 Cor. xi. 19 with Gal. v. 20, where $al\rho\epsilon\sigma\iota s$ is classed with $\delta\iota\chi o\sigma\tau a\sigma\iota a$.)

" Tolosa, tota dolosa," being, as he adds, seldom or never from its foundation free from heresy, fathers handing it on to their sons. The impact came at a time when the Church of Rome was putting forth all its power to extend its spiritual supremacy northward, and the Kingdom of France its territorial domains southward, and it suited their respective interests to unite their forces in a home-crusade against Southern France. Between the upper and nether millstones the body was crushed, but " its soul goes marching on." Its enemies declared it to be rank paganism (Manicheism)* : its adherents the purest form of Christianity (Catharism). An impartial investigation will, we think, show that neither claim can be substantiated. Impartiality, however, is not easily preserved. Most of the documentary evidence which has come down to us is biassed. The Church considered it its sacred duty to destroy all heretical literature as pestiferous : the heretics, equally, the archives of the early inquisitions, whenever they fell into their hands in their few military successes, on the ground that they were dangerous to their members and distortive of their doctrines. " No person," observes Francis Palgrave in his " History of the Anglo-Saxons," " ever can attempt any historical inquiry who does not bring some favourite dogma of his own to the task— some principle which he wishes to support—some position which he is anxious to illustrate or defend, and it is quite useless to lament these tendencies to partiality, since

* Ricchini, editor of Moneta's great work, begins his Dissertation : " Manichaeorum haereseos quae tertio Ecclesiae Seculo ex impuris Ethniorum ac Gnosticorum lacunis Manete Persa antesignato emergens, diu lateque pervagata est, sobolem et propaginem fuisse Catharos seu novos xii et xiii seculi Manichaeos nemo dubitat, qui utriusque Sectae dogmata, mores et disciplinam diligenter contulerit."

they are the very incitements to labour." It is because this is true of many who, with political and ecclesiastical predilections, have sought to confirm them by this controversy, that a fresh endeavour should be made to get at the facts of the case. On the one hand we must avoid reading into Homer what Homer never knew. On the other hand we must carefully precipitate the prose which is in solution in the poetry, and separate historical fact from fanatical fiction.

THE ALBIGENSIAN
HERESY

CHAPTER I

THE SOURCE

THE origin of the Albigensian heresies was not indigenous, but imported, although the raw imports were quickly combined with the home products. Their vigorous growth and wide popularity were due to the peculiarly favourable conditions of the country at the time of their introduction.

§ I. NOT MANICHEAN

The Church commonly labelled the heresy " Manichean," but the label was a libel. The word suited well the purpose of the Church, because the name " Manichean " had had for centuries sinister associations, aroused the utter detestation of the orthodox and brought down upon those accused of it the severest penalties of Church and State. It recalled the conflicts of the early Church with Gnosticism. It exercised a subtle fascination over Augustine, and although he afterwards combated it, yet even as Bishop, according to Julian of Eclanum— no mean critic—" he was not entirely free from its infection." The aggressiveness of Manicheism, albeit characteristically insidious and secretive, had, at the appearance of Catharism, became a spent force. The contrary opinion is based on inference, not historical data. The Dualism of the Manichees was not the Dualism of the Catharists, and there were other differences even more separative. No Manichean writer or leader or emissary has left the slightest trace of his name or influence upon Catharist propaganda. The eagerness with which this weapon was forged by the Church and the success with which it was wielded make us suspicious of its justice. Even Bernard of Clairvaux denies that the Catharists originated from Mani.*

§ 2. NOT PRISCILLIAN

Much the same may be said of the view, less widely held, that Catharism was a resurgence of Priscillianism, of the survival of which we have evidence as late as the beginning of the seventh century. It passed the Pyrenees into France. There was undoubtedly a close connection between Aragon and Toulouse. In their Dualism and Asceticism, in their study and canon† of the Scriptures the two movements had points of resemblance, but this is the utmost that can be said in favour of the theory. The Catharists neither claimed to have had their origin in Spain nor attempted to find there a favourable soil for planting their tenets. The slight support that they received was given for political or family reasons only. They used its nearer valleys and mountains as places of refuge, not spheres of propaganda.

§ 3. NOT DONATIST

The resemblance between the Donatists and Albigenses, in their attitude on the unworthiness of ministers

* Sermones in Cant. LXVI.
† Priscillianists rejected the Pentateuch but highly esteemed the Apocryphal " Ascension of Isaiah," and the " Memoirs of the Apostles."

affecting the validity of sacraments and even of the Church itself, affords no historical ground for the theory that that Schism left any seeds in France to germinate only after several centuries. That Schism was confined to North Africa. Apart from the presence of five Gallic Bishops, or assessors with the Bishop of Rome in the trial, Caecilian *v.* Donatus, ordered by the Emperor in A.D. 313, and the Council held at Arles in the following year, France had no interest in the Donatist controversy. The opposite was the case, for the Gallic Bishops were directed to intervene, and the Council was held in Gaul, because Gaul was immune from it, and its doctrinal isolation presumed an impartial platform for the disputants. Another point of resemblance between Donatists and Albigenses was that both alike objected to the coercive interference of the State in Church affairs.* But this and the unworthiness of ministers are " marks " of a Church which have been discussed in all ages, and are no evidence of historical connection.

§ 4. PARTLY PAULICIAN

We reach firmer ground in seeking a connection between the Catharists and the Paulicians. We cannot go so far as to say with Reinéri, himself once a Catharist, that the movement sprang from Bulgaria and Dalmatia, but there is evidence to show that the Catharists themselves did not dispute *some* affinity. Paulician (corrupted into poplican, publican, etc.)† was an early appellation of the Catharist ; and a comparison of their tenets and organization proves that there was too much in common to be ascribed to mere accident. In the ninth century the Paulicians of Armenia saw that circumstances were favourable for the dissemination of their creed among

* Quid est imperatori cum ecclesia ? (' Optatus,' III, *c.* 3.)
† *v. infra*, p. 17, note.

the Slavonic people. For in the early part of that century the Greek monks, Methodius and Cyril, had converted Bulgaria to Christianity, and its King, Boris, who wished to be on friendly terms with both the Frankish Kingdom and the Byzantine Empire, was baptized, and took the name of Michael after his godfather Michael III, the Byzantine Emperor. A special feature to be remembered in this work of conversion is that these two monks translated the New Testament from the Greek into the Bulgar language, and drew up a liturgy. They relied not only upon the spoken word, but also upon the written word " in a tongue understanded of the people "—a method of evangelization common to the Paulicians, Albigenses and Waldenses. Not only so, but the version current amongst the Western heretics can be shewn to be based upon the Greek and not upon the Vulgate. The Doxology of the Lord's Prayer is found in the New Testament of the Slavs and of the Catharists, derived from the later Greek MSS., but does not occur in the earliest codices or in the Vulgate. In Prov. viii. 22 the Catharists read ἔκτισε (" created ") with the LXX, but the Vulgate (possedit) ἐκτήσατο (" possessed "). The Hebrew קָנָה may be rendered by either, but the former, frequently quoted by the Arians, to the alarm and perplexity of Hilary, against Athanasius, furnished the Church with grounds upon which to base a charge of Arianism against the Catharists. In the archives of the Inquisition of Carcassonne is a Latin version of the Apocryphal Narrative of the Questions of St. John and the Answers of Jesus Christ, at the end of which is a note : " This is a secret document of the heretics of Corcorezio, brought from *Bulgaria* by Nazarius their Bishop, full of errors."

The insistence upon the right of every nation to have the word of God in its own language was a principle common to Paulicians and Catharists, while the Papacy, holding that such a practice contributed to schism as well as heresy, endeavoured to thrust one version, the Latin, upon the whole Church, and refused permission to any but the clergy to read the Scriptures. The Oriental Church was scarcely more compliant. Sergius, of Tavia in Asia Minor, one of the ablest of the apostles of Paulicianism, was won over to the sect by a personal study of the Scriptures which, he had been taught, were to be read only by the clergy.* The story which comes from the Paulicians of Galatia of Asia Minor might be transferred almost word for word to describe similar conversions to Catharism in Gallia of France.

Reverting to Bulgaria, Boris had desired to give Christianity an authoritative and organized position in his dominions, and for this purpose applied to Constantinople for a Bishop. Being refused, he appealed to Rome. But from the Pope he received an even sterner rebuff. However, jealousy gave what justice denied ; for the Patriarch of Constantinople, on hearing of Rome's refusal, altered his tone and gave the King more than he asked, viz. one Archbishop and ten Bishops. We may be certain that these Greek prelates would do nothing to mitigate the antipathy which the Slavo-Greeks would feel towards Rome, and this antipathy deepened into a settled hatred when Rome, later, denied them the right to have the Scriptures in any language but Latin. These troublous times the Paulicians of Armenia, ever zealous propagandists, seized upon for spreading their doctrines. Their asceticism appealed strongly to monks in Bulgaria, Thrace, etc., and in many a monastery Paulicians were welcomed. Persecution also drove them westward, and when in A.D. 969 the Emperor Tzimisces established them in Philippopolis, it was a comparatively easy matter for them to transmit their doctrines along the

* Neander, " Ch. Hist. " Vol. V pp. 346 *seq.* (Bohn).

great trade routes through Bosnia and Dalmatia across and around the Adriatic to Lombardy and France.

At Philippopolis the Paulicians would find a sect called the Euchites already in possession, and, as the latter professed both an absolute and a mitigated Dualism, the two bodies would readily fraternize. The Euchites derived their name from εὐχή, because they regarded prayer as superior to all other Christian duties. But their Slavonic name was Bogomile, which, according to Euthymius, means " God, have pity,"* owing to their frequent use of this phrase in worship. Now " Bogomile " was a name frequently applied to the Catharists, nor did the Catharists repudiate it. Moreover, as will be shewn later, there is a close correspondence between the doctrines and practices of the Paulicians and Bogomiles and those of the Albigenses. These prevailed everywhere throughout the Byzantine Empire, and Crusaders and pilgrims could not fail to come across them. What more probable, then, than that Crusaders straggling and struggling homeward from defeat and disaster in Palestine, to which they had gone at the summons and with the blessing of Holy Church, should lend a sympathetic ear to those whose doctrines were commended by personal asceticism and communal philanthropy ? The blessing had turned to a curse. They returned with the loss not only of health and wealth, but of reverence for and faith in Rome. The Pagan had beaten the Christian. Is it surprising that Catholicity should succumb to suggestions for a new version of Christianity which gave them a plausible and picturesque solution of the conflict between good and evil ? Is it surprising that the soldiers of the conquered Cross should be the channels by which

---

* This has been questioned. The word probably means " The friend of God " (Theophilus). So Gieseler, who says that the complete sentence in Slavonic for " Lord, have mercy " (Kyrie eleison) would be " Gospodine pomilui " (Schmidt Vol. II, pp. 284 *seq.*).

this concept flowed over those very countries from which these disgruntled warriors had set forth ?   Nor must we overlook the pilgrims and the Western mercenaries in the employ of the Eastern Emperors bringing back with them at least information of these sects, even though they did not agree with them.

Again, there is some evidence that the Cathari were prepared to show deference, if not actual subordination, to the Paulicians. At the Synod held A.D. 1167 in St. Felix de Caraman* near Toulouse, at which were present Catharists from Lombardy and Italy, as well as France, Nicetas, the Paulician "Bishop" of Constantinople, attended by request and presided. His ruling that an absolute and not a relative Dualism was the true Creed of Catharism was accepted. The consecration which certain "Bishops" had received from Bulgaria he declared to be invalid, and he reconsecrated them by the imposition of his hands. The "Perfects," fearing lest the Consolamentum† which they had received from such "Bishops" might also be invalid, received the rite again from this "Bishop" of the strict Paulicians. He instituted to the Sees of Toulouse, Carcassonne and the Valley of the Aran three "Bishops" whom these Dioceses had respectively elected. Lastly, he was consulted as to the delimitation of the Dioceses of Toulouse and Carcassonne, and his arbitration was accepted by all parties. His decision was avowedly based upon Eastern and primitive precedent, viz. of the Seven Churches of Asia—not by following the existing municipal and political boundaries of the State, but by considering solely the spiritual interests of the Church. The courtesy of inviting an eminent co-religionist to preside over the Synod's deliberations, and the impartiality to be expected from a disinterested stranger, fail to satisfy the terms of

* A significant connection with Asia Minor.   † *v. infra*, p. 83.

the equation. The authority which Nicetas exercised, acceptance of his consecration and consolamentum in place of the previous ones acknowledged as invalid through a doctrine, erroneous because out of harmony with that of the East, can only be explained on the ground that this Paulician Bishop of the East came to the West as the duly accredited representative of a foster-mother to her daughter Churches.

The title by which the heretics were most widely known was that of Cathari. Unquestionably* derived from καθαρός, "pure," it points to Eastern associations. First met with in the second half of the twelfth century, it is the only appellation used of the heretics by Reinéri and Moneta.

That a Gnostic element, undefined and indefinable, underlay and mingled with the Catholicism of the working classes cannot be denied, and if we can identify the sources of one or two strong streams feeding the Albigensian heresy, these do not necessarily exclude others whose sources evade us. In A.D. 890 Agobard, Archbishop of Lyons, discovered Gnostic elements in his antiphonary. The Declaration of Belief which a century later (A.D. 991) Gerbert published on his appointment to the Archbishopric of Rheims was obviously called forth by the prevalence of Docetic and Dualistic teaching in his Province : " I believe that Christ was the Son of God, that He took a human form from His mother, and in that body suffered, died and rose again. I believe that one and the same God was the originator of both the Old and New Testaments, that Satan was not

---

* In Lombardy called Gazari. Mosheim thought Gazari to be the original form (and Cathari a corruption) from Gazar, the ancient Chersonese of the Taurus. But there is nothing to show there were Dualists there. Neander, while deriving Gazzari from the same place, distinguishes them from Cathari. Ketzer is the common German word for " heretic."

originally evil, but had fallen into evil ; that our present body and no other would rise again ; that marriage and eating meat were both allowable."

In A.D. 1016 an *Armenian* anchorite was detected in Rome and denounced as a heretic, and scarcely escaped with his life. As " Armenian " became synonymous with heretic, we may assume that Armenians were frequent visitors to other places in the West, and that their heresy was Paulician.

§ 5. PARTLY INDIGENOUS

It is not therefore to Spain or Africa that we must look for the origin of the Albigensian heresy, but rather to the East, for in that direction the names Manichean, Bogomile, Bulgar, Paulician, Poplican* and Catharist point, but we can only speak in generalities. We cannot say of this heresy : " In the year —— a band of missioners under —— came to France to convert it to Catharism," as we can say of the English Church : " In the year 597 a band of missioners under Augustine came to England to convert it to Christianity." When we have stretched our historical data to their utmost capacity, when we have made full allowance for the devastation wrought by friend and foe—by friend in the destruction of the records against themselves of the Inquisition, by foe in the destruction of heretical literature—we are convinced that the imports from the East fail in quantity and quality to account for the Albigensian heresies as we find them in full vigour and variety. Their germs might have been found almost

* To the several solutions proposed of this word (*v.* Du Cange *s.v.*), I would add the suggestion that it is a popular abbreviation of Philippopolicani, Philippopolis being the most active and most western centre of Paulician propagandism. Such popular abbreviations of cumbersome words are found in all languages.

anywhere in Western Christendom in the Middle Ages, but the stimulus to growth came not from without, but from within. It was a spontaneous outburst of a profound discontent with a Church which by its Ultramontanism opposed all national independence, and by its unspirituality forfeited all respect for its creed. Just as the Church turned back to Aristotelian and Platonic philosophy to illuminate the mystical element—the relationship between the outward and the inward—in its own entity and in its Sacraments—a philosophy which had long lain dormant in her midst—so the Catharists turned back to Dualistic Gnosticism to illuminate the origin of good and evil, and its bearing upon ecclesiastical organization. But whereas the students of the North were attracted to dialectics, the light-hearted of the South of France were drawn to picturesque myths. It was an age when men everywhere, and especially in France, were devoting themselves to a reconsideration of the Church, in its essence, its doctrines and its activities ; but while the Church forced facts to suit philosophic theories, the Catharists adopted and devised Dualistic theories to suit the facts. The Church claimed that its doctrines such as that of the Holy Roman Empire or of Transubstantiation, were not new, but inherent in and developed from the authority and teaching of its Divine Head. The Catharists maintained that they were corruptions and profanities, weeds not fruit, and only when they were swept away would the Christian Church be pure and therefore powerful. How far circumstances favoured them falls now to be considered.

CHAPTER II

THE SOIL

§ I. GALATIAN

IN order to understand the situation, political and ecclesiastical, in Southern France we must bear in mind that the Gauls of the West and the Galatae of the East were of the same stock, and that each branch, though several nations intervened, retained unimpaired its racial characteristics. Galli, Galatae, Keltae are but different forms of the same word. Livy would speak of Gauls in the East ; Polybius of Galatians in the West. The Gauls were a warm-hearted people, but unstable in their friendships, impetuous and courageous in war, but unable to wear down a foe by stubborn endurance. As Cæsar noticed : " sunt in consiliis capiendis mobiles, et novis plerumque rebus student ; " an opinion endorsed in modern times by one of their own nation—Thierry : " Une bravoure personnelle que rien n'égale chez les peuples anciens—un esprit franc, impétueux, ouvert à toutes les impressions, éminemment intelligent—mais, à côté de cela, une mobilité extrême, point de constance, une répugnance marquée aux idées de discipline et d'ordre." To these traits may be added vivid imagination, a fondness for song and poetry, a love of nature so intimate that allegory became reality.

Gaul had become one of the perpetual conquests of Rome and had submitted to its governmental system, but nothing could eradicate its racial peculiarities. The

Gaul was an individualist, the Roman an imperialist, and hence the Gaul might be conquered, but never destroyed. Now this imperialism which the Church took over from the State was developed vigorously and rapidly under Pope Gregory VII and his successors, and the insistence of it aroused a corresponding reaction in Gaulish nationalism. The Church had condemned Nominalism as inimical to Catholic unity, and had adopted the opposite scholastic theory of Realism as most agreeable to the theory of the Holy Roman Empire. This theory, however, now declared to be a dogma of the Catholic faith, struck at the root of national and individual independence. Such an independence France had constantly shewn, and it may be traced not only to the racial antipathy between Gaul and Pelagian, but to the fact that Western Gaul had never lost touch with its Eastern kin. Its Christianity from the earliest times was on Eastern rather than Western lines. Its monasticism was of the Oriental type. The letter which the Christians of Gaul in A.D. 177, describing the sufferings and deaths of the martyrs in the persecution, sent to " the brethren in Asia and Phrygia, having the same faith and hope of redemption with us," can only be explained on the assumption that they were of the same kith and kin. In fact, one of the martyrs, Alexander, was a Phrygian.* The Gallican Liturgy was Eastern (Ephesian), not Western.

§ 2. SLAVONIC

The spirit of independence which pervaded Southern France would be strengthened by its constant communication with Slavonia, for the Slavs, according to

---

* Οἱ ἐν Βιέννῃ καὶ Λουγδούνῳ τῆς Γαλλίας παροικοῦντες δοῦλοι Χριστοῦ, τοῖς κατὰ τὴν Ἀσίαν καὶ Φρυγίαν τὴν αὐτὴν τῆς ἀπολυτρώσεως ἡμῖν πίστιν καὶ ἐλπίδα ἔχουσιν ἀδελφοῖς. (Euseb., H.E., v. 1.)

Procopius, had the same national characteristics. " They
are not ruled by one man, but from the most ancient times
have been under a democracy. In favourable and unfavourable situations all their affairs are placed before a
common council." The " ' Times ' History of the World "
says : " The Slavs are characterised by a vivacity, a
warmth, a mobility, a petulance, an exuberance not
always found in the same degree among even the people
of the South. Among the Slavs of purer blood these
characteristics have marked their political life with a
mobile, inconstant and anarchical spirit. . . . The dis-
tinguishing faculty of the race is a certain flexibility and
elasticity of temperament and character which render it
adaptable to the reception and the reproduction of all
sorts of diverse ideas." This likeness of temperament
would naturally draw two nations together and account
for the readiness with which the Gallican mind absorbed
Slavonic propaganda.

§ 3. NATIVE

The country had been early converted to Christianity,
and the dominant form of Christianity was now Roman.
But when we speak of a country being " converted "
in the Middle Ages, we must regard the statement with
considerable qualifications. Conversions were often
political conveniences, rather than personal convictions.
The people followed their chiefs, accepted the Church's
ministrations and attended her services, but knew next
to nothing of Christian truth. In France two things
contributed to this ignorance : (*a*) the official language
of the Church being different from that of the people ;
(*b*) the slackness and refusal of the Church in providing
services and sermons in a language which the people
understood.

Between the middle of the eighth and ninth centuries

Latin was the language only of the learned and officials ;
the mass of the people ceased to understand it. Latin
was sacrosanct, and to address God in any other language
was profane. Hence the Church lost its spiritual hold
upon the masses. " The hungry sheep looked up and
were not fed." So serious was the situation that Charlemagne summoned five Councils at five different places,
the most Southern being Arles, and ordered the Bishops
to use the vulgar tongue in the instruction of their
flocks. From this it is clear that the Bishops and Clergy
were bilingual, but deliberately abstained from adopting
in their pastoral work a language which their people
could understand ; even the Bible was a closed book.
The heretics, on the contrary, were most zealous in
supplying this want, particularly the Waldenses. Not
only did they translate the whole of the New Testament
and parts of the Old, but added notes embodying Sen-
tentiae or opinions of the Fathers. They contended
that prayers in an unknown tongue did not profit. They
knew by heart large portions of Holy Scripture* and
readily quoted it in their discussions with the Church.
The Catharists also had composed a little work called
" Perpendiculum Scientiarum," or " Plummet of Knowledge " (cf. Is. xxviii. 17), consisting of passages of
Scripture whereby Catholicism might be easily and
readily tested. Not until the eleventh century do we
come across in the West any translation into the vulgar
tongue by the Church, and then only of Legends of
Saints in the dialect of Rouen. In Southern France the
vernacular which ultimately emerged was known as
Langue D'Oc, and sometimes Provençal. "In its
rise Provençal literature stands completely by itself,
and in its development it long continued to be

---

* Reinéri Saccho says he knew an ignorant rustic who could recite
the book of Job word for word.

absolutely original. This literature took a poetic
form, and this poetry, unlike classical poetry, is
rhymed." No class of literature is more easily remembered than rhymed verse in common speech.
The results of it, therefore, need not cause us surprise.
It produced a sense of unity, of comradeship. Latin
might be the language of the Church, but this was the
language of the people. Its growth created a cleavage
between Church and people, which the former sought
to bridge by giving the latter accounts of miracles and
legends in verse and prose in the Romance language,
and by permitting them to sing songs of their own com-
position—and not necessarily sacred or even modest
songs—in the Churches.* But the experiment or concession only served to secularize religion, and turned
the services into amusements. Nor was it in accord
with the real policy of Catholicism which was to prevent
the people generally from forming their own opinions
of Christianity by an independent study of the Scriptures
—a policy which to the Gallican temperament would be
particularly odious and exasperating.†

§ 4. SECULAR ELEMENTS

Secular causes also account for the growing unpopularity of the Church. On the one hand the seigneurs
resented the increasing wealth and land encroachments of
Bishops and Abbots. " In the eleventh century the fear
of the approaching final judgment and the belief in the

* In sanctorum vigiliis in ecclesiis historicae (=histrionicae) salta-
tiones, obsceni motus seu choreae fiunt . . . dicuntur amatoria
carmina vel cantilenae ibidem (Council of Avignon, Canon xvii, A.D.
1209).

† Prohibemus—ne libros Veteris Testamenti aut Novi laici permit-
tantur habere : nisi forte psalterium vel breviarium pro divinis officiis,
aut horas beatae Mariae aliquis ex devotione habere velit. Sed ne
praemissos libros habeant in vulgari translatos arctissime inhibemus
(Council of Toulouse, Canon XIV, A.D. 1229).

speedy dissolution of the world spread throughout all
Europe. Some bestowed the whole of their possessions
on the Church."* But when the donors recovered from
their alarm, they regretted their sacrifice, and their
descendants would be provoked every day at the sight
of others in enjoyment of their ancestral lands. Moreover, the break-up of Charlemagne's vast kingdom threw
great power into the hands of the Dukes and Counts.
In their own domains they were practically autocrats.
The only check upon their sovereignty came from the
Church, whose Bishops and Abbots were often able to
protect themselves by their own routiers or by ecclesiastical penalties, such as excommunication. But the
lords countered this by thrusting their own nominees,
often their own relations, into the most powerful and
lucrative offices of the Church, or by keeping them
vacant and appropriating their revenues. A semblance
of legality was thrown over this practice by the fact
that " the Bishoprics being secular fiefs, their occupants
were bound to the performance of feudal service," and
the investiture into the temporalities of the office belonged
to the sovereign. Thus the freedom of the Church in
the election and appointment of her officers was curtailed.

§ 5. COMMERCE

On the other hand, the increase of commercial prosperity
broke down the feudal system. The merchants took
advantage of the poverty of the Counts through constant
wars by obtaining in exchange for loans certain privileges
which, by charter, settled into the inalienable rights of
the ville franche. They built for themselves fortified
houses in the towns, and from them laughed to scorn
the threats of the seigneurs. Their enterprise was con-

* Hegel's " Philosophy of History," Pt. IV, Sect. II.

stantly bringing money into the country : the non-productive Church was constantly sending it out. Trade with foreign countries created in commercial and industrial circles a sense of independence, and their enlarged outlook gave birth to a religious tolerance favourable to doctrines other than, or in addition to, those of Catholicism. Thus Peter Waldo, the merchant of Lyons, was moved to devote his wealth to disseminate the Word of God as freely as he disposed of his merchandise. These goods had to be made, and the actual manufacturers, especially the weavers, shared in the general prosperity and imbibed this freedom of thought. Erasmus' great wish, that the weaver might warble the Scriptures at his loom,* was anticipated by three centuries by the Albigenses, and especially by the Waldenses. So widely did heresy spread among these textile workers that heretic and tesserand became synonymous. At Cordes a nominal factory was set up, but in reality a theological school for instruction in Catharism.†

§ 6. LITERATURE

Although it suited the purpose of the Church to regard them as " unlearned and ignorant men," it was from the people that the Provençal literature emanated. The bourgeoisie encouraged poetry and art. The industrial classes turned in contempt from the stupid and impossible stories of saints to a personal study of the Scriptures and their patristic explanations. The Poor Men of Lyons were poor in spirit, not in pocket. Business

* Paracelsus, " Works," Vol. IV, p. 141.
† Prob. in A.D. 1212, when the inhabitants fled to Cordes (then a mere hunting-box of the Counts of Toulouse) from St. Marcel, which was destroyed by Simon de Montfort. The date usually assigned to the founding of Cordes, viz. 1222, is wrong. *See* " Records of the Académie imperiale des Sciences, Toulouse," Series 6, Vol. V. For this reference I am indebted to my friend, Col. de Cordes.

ability and training enabled them to organize their movement on lines that were both flexible and compact, and their wealth supported their officers. Clerks could copy out their pamphlets, and their colporteurs or travellers could distribute them. At the beginning of the thirteenth century the Marquis of Montferrand, in Auvergne, just before his death, burnt a great quantity of books, especially those of Albigensian propaganda, which he had been collecting for forty years. (Stephen de Belleville, 85.) The Provençal, Arnauld, was a most prolific writer, and sold or gave to the Catholics little books deriding the saints of the Church. Moneta de Cremona, in his great work against the Albigenses, declares that he drew his information of their doctrines from their own writings, and quotes largely from a teacher called Tetricus, a dialectician and intepreter of the Bible. Tetricus was probably that William who was Canon of Nevers, returned to Toulouse in 1201, under the name of Theodoric, and was held in great esteem by the Albigenses for his knowledge.*

§ 7. MORAL AND SPIRITUAL ELEMENTS

But of all the causes of the unpopularity of the Church the unworthy lives of the clergy was the most potent, the evidence for which comes less from the accusations of the heretics than from the confessions of the Church itself. To allow immodest songs, composed by the people, to be sung in Church is sufficiently significant of the low standard of the clerical mind ; but instances are given of the clergy themselves composing these songs. Agobard, Bishop of Lyons, found there a service-book compiled by an assistant Bishop (*chorepiscopus*) so

* Nearly a century before this (*v. infra*) Henry, the successor of Peter de Bruis, wrote a book which Peter Venerabilis had seen himself, setting forth the several heads of the heresy.

indecent that he could not read it without a blush. The
decrees of Councils throw a strong light upon the luxurious
and worldly lives of Bishops and Clergy—their costly
clothes, painted saddles and gold-mounted reins, joining
in games of chance, their habit of swearing, and allowing
others to swear at them without reproof, welcoming to
their tables strolling players, hearing Mattins in bed,
being frivolous when saying the Offices, excommunicating
persons wrongfully, simony, tolerating clerical con-
cubinage, dispensing with banns, celebrating secret
marriages, quashing wills. These are not the slanders
of heretics, but the testimony of the Church in formal
assembly. The Pope, Innocent III, is equally scandalized.
Writing of the Archbishop of Narbonne and its clergy,
he exclaims : " Blind ! dumb dogs that cannot bark !
Simoniacs who sell justice, absolve the rich and condemn
the poor ! They do not keep even the laws of the Church.
They accumulate benefices and entrust the priesthood
and ecclesiastical dignities to unworthy priests and
illiterate children. Hence the insolence of the heretics ;
hence the contempt of nobles and people for God and His
Church. In this region prelates are the laughing stock
of the laity. And the cause of all the evil is the Archbishop of Narbonne. He knows no other god than
money. His heart is a bank. During the ten years
he has been in office he has never once visited his Province, not even his own Diocese. He took five hundred
golden pennies for consecrating the Bishop of Maguelonne,
and when we asked him to raise subsidies for the Christians
in the East he refused. When a Church falls vacant, he
refrains from nominating an incumbent, and appropriates
the income. For the same reason he has reduced by half
the number of canons (eighteen) and kept the arch-
deaconries vacant. In his Diocese monks and canons
regular have renounced their Order and married wives ;

they have become money-lenders, lawyers, jugglers and doctors." Even Papal Legates, sent to combat heresy, conformed to the same luxurious mode of life, and called down upon themselves the severe reproofs of Bishop Diego and Prior Dominic. Gaucelin Faidit wrote a play, called " The Heresy of the Priests," in which he flung back upon the Clergy the charges which they brought against the Cathari. It was acted with much applause before Boniface, Marquis of Montferrat, the friend of Raymond VI, Count of Toulouse (A.D. 1193–1202). Nor, indeed, could it be expected that those who shewed themselves so indifferent to the sacredness of their calling would do other than encourage violations of their prerogatives by the powers of this world. The Counts, therefore, according to Godfrey's Chronicle, handed over Churches to stupid persons or to their own relations, and that simoniacally. Such people shew themselves to be hirelings, shearing the sheep and not attending to their infirmities, and—what is worse—encouraging in sin those whom they ought to correct. The Bishops went about their dioceses exacting illegal taxes and exchanging procurations for indulgences.

In contrast to all this was the life and character of the Catharists—for we may dismiss as incapable of proof the charges of extinguished lights, promiscuous intercourse, etc., which were but a rechauffé of the charges made against the early Christians. Catharism, which means Puritanism, was a constant and conspicuous protest to an age and people characterized by a *joie de vivre*. The asceticism of the " Perfect " in particular went beyond that of the severest monasticism, for they eschewed meat always, and not merely at certain times of the year, as well as all food produced by generation Their relationship of the sexes was ultra-strict. Their word was their bond, and their religion forbade them to mar it with an oath. They possessed no money, and were supported by the community. Their simplicity and modesty in dress, their frugality, their industry, their honesty, kindled the respect, even the reverence, of the masses.* No hardships or dangers daunted their missionary ardour. When the Church attacked the heretics by means other than by fire and sword, she failed until the Dominicans copied their methods and the Franciscans their manners.

* Reinéri Saccho, a former Catharist (but not, as he is careful to point out, a Waldensian) and afterward an Inquisitor, says the heretics were distinguished by their conduct and conversation : they were sedate, modest, had no pride in clothes, did not carry on business dishonestly, did not multiply riches, did not go to taverns, dances, etc. ; were chaste, especially the Leonists, temperate in meat and drink, not given to anger, always at work, teaching and learning, and therefore prayed little, went to Church, but only to catch the preacher in his discourse ; precise and moderate in language. A man swam the River Ibis every night in winter to make one convert.

CHAPTER III

THE SEED

W E are now in a position to study more closely the documents from which an estimate may be formed of the beliefs and practices of those whom the Church exerted its full strength to destroy. Our task is not a simple one, because, as already stated, there was not one heresy, but many, and we are dependent for our knowledge of their tenets almost entirely upon their enemies whose *odium theologicum* discounts their trustworthiness.

§ I. EYMERIC

It may simplify our task if we set down the fourteen heads under which the Inquisitor Eymeric in his " Directorium Inquisitorum "* classifies what he calls " *recentiorum* Manicheorum errores."

(1) They assert and confess that there are two Gods or two Lords, viz. a good God, and an evil Creator of all things visible and material ; declaring that these things were not made by God our heavenly Father . . . but by a wicked devil, even Satan . . . and so they assume two Creators, viz. God and the Devil ; and two Creations, viz. one of immaterial and invisible things, the other of visible and material.

(2) They imagine that there are two Churches, one good, which they say is their own sect, and declare to

* Part II, pp. 273, 274, Venice.

be the Church of Jesus Christ ; the other, however, they call an evil Church, which they say is the Church of Rome.

(3) All grades, orders, ordinances and statutes of the Church they despise and ignore, and all who hold the Faith they call heretics and deluded, and positively assert (*dogmatizant*) that nobody can be saved by the faith (*in fide*) of the Roman Church.

(4) All the Sacraments of the Roman Church of our Lord Jesus Christ, viz. the Eucharist, and Baptism performed with material water, also Confirmation and Orders and Extreme Unction and Penance (*poenitentia*) and Matrimony, all and singular, they assert to be vain and useless.

(5) They invent, instead of holy Baptism in water, another *spiritual* Baptism, which they call the Consolation (*consolamentum*)* of the Holy Spirit.

(6) They invent, instead of the consecrated bread of the Eucharist of the Body of Christ, a certain bread, which they call " blessed bread," or " bread of holy prayer," which, holding in their hands, they bless according to their rite, and break and distribute to their fellow-believers seated.

(7) Instead of the Sacrament of Penance they say that their sect receives and holds a true Penance (*poenitentia*), and to those holding the said sect and order, whether they be in health or sickness, all sins are forgiven (*dimissa*), and that such persons are absolved from all their sins without any other satisfaction, asserting that they themselves have over these the same and as great power as had Peter and Paul and the other Apostles . . . saying that the confession of sins which is made to the priests of the Roman Church is of no avail whatever for salvation, and that neither the Pope nor any

* *v. infra*, p. 83.

other person of the Roman Church has power to absolve anyone from his sins.

(8) Instead of the Sacrament of carnal Matrimony between man and woman, they invent a spiritual Matrimony between the soul and God, viz. when the heretics themselves, the perfect or consoled (*perfecti seu consolati*), receive anyone into their sect and order.

(9) They deny the Incarnation of our Lord Jesus Christ from Mary ever virgin, asserting that He had not a true human body, etc., but that all things were done figuratively (*in similitudinem*).

(10) They deny that the Blessed Virgin Mary was the true mother of our Lord Jesus Christ ; they deny also that she was a woman of flesh (*carnalem*). But they say their sect and order is the Virgin Mary, and that true penance (*poenitentia*) is a chaste virgin who bears sons of God when they are received into their sect and order.

(11) They deny the future resurrection of human bodies, imagining, instead, certain spiritual bodies.

(12) They say that a man ought to eat or touch neither meat nor cheese nor eggs, nor anything which is born of the flesh by way of generation or intercourse.

(13) They say and believe that in brutes and even in birds there are those spirits which go forth from the bodies of men when they have not been received into their sect and order by imposition of hands, according to their rite, and that they pass from one body into another ; wherefore they themselves do not eat or kill any animal or anything that flies.

(14) They say that a man ought never to touch a woman.

§ 2. ADEMAR

The earliest mention of the heterodox as *Manichees* is found in Ademar, a noble of Aquitaine, who says : " Shortly afterwards (A.D. 1018) there arose throughout

Aquitaine Manichees, seducing the people. They denied Baptism and the Cross, and whatever is of sound doctrine. Abstaining from food, they appeared like monks and feigned chastity, but amongst themselves they indulged in every luxury and were the messengers of Anti-Christ, and have caused many to err from the faith."*

§ 3. COUNCIL OF ORLEANS

These " Manichees " may have fled from the theological school at Orleans where heresy had been detected and punished only the year before, although neither Glaber Radulf † nor Agono, of the monastery of St. Peter's, Chartres,‡ both contemporaries, denominates them Manichees. The proceedings of the Council of Orleans, though beyond our area, is of interest to us, because of the eminence and influence of its theological school, and also because the Queen, Constance, was daughter of Raymond of Toulouse, she having married Robert after he had been compelled to divorce his first wife, Bertha. The heresy, by whatever name it reached or left Orleans, probably affected Southern France, for it is stated that the heresy was brought into Gaul by an *Italian* woman " by whom many in *many* parts were corrupted." The " depravity " of the heretics was spread secretly, and was only disclosed to the King by a nobleman of Normandy, named Arefast, who became acquainted with the existence of the heresy through a young ecclesiastic, Heribert. At the Council (A.D. 1022) which the King summoned, and which consisted of many Bishops, Abbots and *laymen*,§ the three ringleaders, Stephen, the Queen's Confessor, Heribert, who had filled the post of ambassador

* Chronicle, Migne's " Patrol," Tom. 141, p. 63.
† " History," Book III, Chap. 8.
‡ D'Achery " Spicilegium," Vol. I, p. 604.
§ Incidentally we may note the fact of a Council called to decide a matter of faith presided over by a layman, with laymen as co-judges with ecclesiastics.

to the King of France, and Lisois, all famous for their
learning, holiness and generosity, declared that every-
thing in the Old and New Testaments about the Blessed
Trinity, although authority supported it by signs and
wonders and ancient witnesses, was nonsense ; that
heaven and earth never had an author, and are eternal ;
that Jesus Christ was not born of the Virgin Mary, did
not suffer for men, was not placed in the sepulchre, and
did not rise again from the dead ; that there is no washing
away of sins in Baptism ; that there is no sacrament of
the Body and Blood of Christ at the consecration by a
priest ; intercessions of saints, martyrs and confessors
are valueless.   Arefast, the informer, said he asked
wherein then he could rest his hope of salvation ; he was
invited to submit to their imposition of hands, then he
would be pure from all sin, and be filled with the Holy
Spirit Who would teach him the depths and true meaning
(*profunditatem et veram dignitatem*) of all the Scriptures
without any reserve. He would see visions of Angels who
would always help him, and God his Friend (*comes*)
would never let him want for anything.*   They were
like the Epicureans, and did not believe that flagitious
pleasures would be punished, or that piety and righteousness—the wealth of Christians—would receive ever-
lasting reward.   Arefast also brings against them the
odious charges of extinguished lights and promiscuous
intercourse ; the children thus begotten were solemnly
burnt the day after their birth, their ashes preserved and
given to the dying as a Viaticum.   Threatened with
death by fire, they boasted that they would escape
from the flames. Sentenced to death, the King feared
lest they should be killed in the Church and commanded
Queen Constance to stand on guard at the door. But
the Queen herself got out of hand, for as the condemned

* Agono.

heretics came forth she gouged out (*eruit*) with a staff the eye of Stephen, her late confessor. As soon as they felt the fire, they cried out that they had been deceived by the Devil, and that the God and Lord of the universe, Whom they had blasphemed, was punishing them with torture temporal and eternal. Some of the bystanders were deeply moved and endeavoured to rescue them, but in vain. The number who perished varies between fourteen and ten. " A like fate met others who held a like faith," says Glaber, " and thus the Catholic faith was vindicated and everywhere shone more brightly."

The Council's investigations also brought to light the fact that a Canon of Orleans, and Precentor, called Theodotus (*Dieudonné*), had three years before died in heresy, although he pretended to live and die in the communion of the Church. On this deception being discovered, his body was exhumed by order of Bishop Odalric and thrown away. It will be noted that the Council does not call them Manichees or any other name. In fact, with the exception of Ademar, no one for nearly a century identifies the heretics with Manicheism. They are not labelled at the Council of Charroux in A.D. 1028 (or 1031). At the Council of Rheims in A.D. 1049 they are vaguely spoken of as " new heretics who have arisen in France." The Council of Toulouse in A.D. 1056 condemned in its thirteenth Canon certain heretics, but does not specify their errors. In A.D. 1110 in the Diocese of Albi, Bishop Sicard and Godfrey of Muret, Abbot of Castres, attempted to seize some heretics already excommunicated, but were prevented by nobles and people ; but they are only colourlessly described as :

Astricti Satanae qui sunt anathemate diro,
Noluntque absolvi restituique Deo.*

* " Chron. epis. Albig. et Abbot. Cast.," D'Achery, III, 572. Radulf Ardens, however, preacher of William IX, Duke of Aquitaine (d. 1137), speaks of the heretics as Manichees (" Sermons," p. 325), *v. infra*, p. 39.

§ 4. COUNCIL OF TOULOUSE

Another Council held at Toulouse in A.D. 1119, presided over by the Pope, Callistus III, is more precise, but does not denominate them. By its third Canon it enacted : " Moreover, those who, pretending to a sort of religion, condemn the Sacrament of the Body and Blood of the Lord, the Baptism of children, the priesthood and other ecclesiastical orders and the compacts of lawful marriage, we expel from the Church of God as heretics and condemn them, and enjoin upon the secular powers (*exteras potestates*) to restrain them. In the bonds of this same sentence we include their defenders until they recant."

§ 5. PETER DE BRUIS

A new heresiarch now comes upon the scene in the person of Peter de Bruis, of whom nothing previous is known, except that according to Alfonso à Castro he was a Gaul of Narbonne. We first hear of him from Maurice de Montboissier, better known as Petrus Venerabilis, Abbot of Cluny, who addressed an open letter " to the lords, fathers and masters of the Church of God, the Archbishops of Arles and Embrun " and certain Bishops. As the Abbot died in A.D. 1126(7), and the heresiarch laboured for twenty years in promulgating his teaching, he was contemporary with the Council of Toulouse of A.D. 1119,* and its condemnation may have been directed in part against his followers, who were called Petrobrusians. The letter of the Abbot has a preface which is not his, but which was written after his death. This preface sums up the tenets of the Petrobrusians under five heads :

(1) They deny that little children under years of

* Peter himself was dead by A.D. 1121. *v*. Abelard, opp. p. 1066.

discretion (*intelligibilem aetatem*) can be saved by the baptism of Christ, and another's faith cannot benefit those who cannot use their own . . . for the Lord said, " Whosoever *believed* and was baptized was saved."

(2) Temples and Churches ought not to be built, and those already built ought to be pulled down, and sacred places for praying were not necessary to Christians, since equally in tavern or church, in market or temple, before altar or stall, God, when called upon, hears and hearkens to those who deserve.

(3) All holy crosses should be broken up and burnt, since that instrument by which Christ was so fearfully tortured and so cruelly put to death was not worthy of adoration, veneration or any other worship, but in revenge for His torments and death should be dishonoured with every kind of infamy, struck with swords and burnt.

(4) Not only do they deny the truth of the Body and Blood of the Lord in the Sacrament daily and continually offered up in the Church, but declare that it is absolutely nothing and ought not to be offered to God.

(5) They deride sacrifices, prayers, alms and other good things done by the faithful living for the faithful departed, and affirm that these things cannot help any of the dead in the smallest degree.* Also " they say God is mocked by Church hymns, because He delights in pious desires, and cannot be summoned by loud voices or appeased by musical notes."†

In the letter itself Peter Venerabilis points out to the prelates that in their parts the people were re-baptized, churches profaned, altars thrown down, crosses burnt. Meat was publicly eaten on the very day of the Lord's Passion, priests were scourged, monks imprisoned and compelled by terrors and tortures to marry. " The

---

* Migne, " Patrol," Tom. 189, p. 719.   † *Ibid.*, p. 1079.

heads, indeed, of these pests by God's help as well as by
the aid of Catholic princes you have driven out of your
territories. But the slippery serpent, gliding out of your
territories, or rather driven out by your prosecution,
has betaken itself to the Province of Narbonne, and
whereas with you it used to whisper in deserts and
hamlets in fear, it now preaches boldly in great meetings
and crowded cities. But let the most distant shores of
the swift Rhone and the champaign adjacent to Toulouse,
and the city itself, more populous than its neighbours,
drive out this opinion ; for the better informed the city
is, the more cautious it ought to be against false dogma."
Peter de Bruis was burnt by the faithful in revenge for
the crosses which he had burnt.

§ 6. HENRY OF CLUNY

But " the blood of the martyrs is the seed of the
Church," whether that Church be true or false, and the
mantle of Peter de Bruis fell strangely upon Henry, a
fellow monk at Cluny of Peter Venerabilis. Henry,
" haeres nequitiae ejus," with many others " doctrinam
diabolicam non quidem emendavit sed immutavit,"
and wrote it down in a volume which Peter himself
had seen, and that not under five heads, but several.
" Haeres," however, must be loosely interpreted with
regard to both time and teaching. For Henry had
already been wonderfully successful as a revivalist else-
where, and his teaching did not entirely coincide with
that of Peter de Bruis. For instance, whereas the latter
burnt the cross, Henry had one carried before him and
his followers when he entered towns and villages, and
made it the emblem and inspiration of a life of self-
denial, to which his own monastic training would
predispose him. So far from calling for the destruction
of sacred buildings, he used them, when he obtained

permission—as he did from Bishop Hildebert—for his mission preaching. He insisted upon the celibacy of the clergy, but regulated in minute detail the marriage of the laity. In fact, it is not easy to see how his teaching could be called heretical, unless it were his opposition to saint-worship, and doubtless he would have been allowed to move about freely had he not denounced the luxurious lives of the clergy and exposed them to the contempt and insults of the people. Arrested in A.D. 1134 he was condemned for heresy at the Council of Pisa, and imprisoned there ; but he was released and returned to France, where he laboured in and around Toulouse and Albi, and met with remarkable success, not only amongst the laity, but even amongst the clergy ; so much so, indeed, that the Churches were emptied of both, in order that priest and people might join the sect, which, after its leader, was called Henricians. Not until A.D. 1148 was he finally suppressed. Brought before a Council at Rheims he was sentenced to imprisonment for life, a punishment which goes to shew that he was not regarded as a heretic, but as a firebrand whose inflammatory activity must, for the peace of the Church, be extinguished. Reform of life rather than reform of doctrine was the aim of Henry's mission.

§ 7. RALPH ARDENS

But although that mission was successful, it did not absorb all the anti-church movements. The Dualistic creed still obtained in many parts of Southern France, as Radulf Ardens* (" Sermons," p. 325) declared : " Such to-day, my brethren, are the Manichean heretics, for

* Preacher of William IX, Duke of Aquitaine. This was *c.* A.D. 1101. Thirteen years later (A.D. 1114) Robert of Arbrisselles, summoned by the Bp. Amelius to Toulouse, by his eloquence and reasoning brought back many into the fold of the Church (Percin, II, 3).

they have defiled our fatherland of Agen. They falsely assert that they keep to the Apostolic life, saying that they do not lie or swear at all ; on the pretence of abstinence and continence they condemn flesh-food and marriage. They say that it is as great a sin to approach a wife as it is a mother or daughter. They condemn the Old Testament, and receive only some parts of the New. But what is more serious is they preach that there are two authors of Nature (*rerum*), God the author of things invisible, and the Devil the author of things visible. Hence, they secretly worship the Devil, because they believe him to be the creator of their body. They say that the Sacrament of the Altar is plain (*purum*) bread. They deny Baptism. They preach that no one can be saved except by their hands. They deny also the resurrection of the body."

§ 8. BERNARD OF CLAIRVAUX

Bernard of Clairvaux (b. A.D. 1091), however, refuses to connect the heretics with any human founder, Mani, Peter de Bruis, or Henry. " These " (heretics), he exclaims,* " are sheep in appearance (*habitu*), foxes in cunning, wolves in cruelty. They are rustics, ignorant and utterly despicable, but you must not deal with them carelessly. . . . They prohibit marriage, they abstain from food. The Manicheans had Mani for chief and instructor, the Arians Arius, etc. By what name or title do you think you can call these ? By none, for their heresy is not of man, and they did not receive it through man. It is by the deceit of devils. . . . Still some differ from the rest, and profess that marriage should be contracted only between bachelors and virgins (*inter solos virgines*). They deny that the fire of purgatory remains after death."

* " Sermones in Cantica," LXVI (Song of Solomon, ii, 15).

§ 9. COUNCIL OF TOURS

But something more official, more imposing than separate and isolated denunciations and condemnations of individuals was demanded by reason of the rapid and extensive growth of these heresies. Accordingly a Council met at Tours in A.D. 1163, the title of the fourth Canon of which is : " That all should avoid the company (*consortium*) of the Albigensian heretics." Here, for the first time, I believe, we meet with the name Albigenses as a distinct religious sect. The heresy is, if the title is authentic, directly and officially connected with these people, although Toulouse, and not Albi, is specifically mentioned in the Canon itself. The fourth Canon says : " In the parts of Toulouse a damnable heresy has lately arisen, and like a canker is slowly diffusing itself into the neighbouring localities, and has already infected Gascony* and many other provinces. The Bishops and Priests of the Lord in those parts we enjoin to be on their guard and under threat of anathema forbid anyone

---

* This heresy cannot be identified with that of the Publicani, if William of Newbury can be trusted in his account of the Council of Oxford, A.D. 1160. (L. ii. cap. xiii.) " At the same time there came into England certain wayfarers (*erronei*), believed to be of that body commonly called Publicani. These, doubtless, had their origin *in Gascony* from an author unknown, and had poured the poison of their perfidy into many regions. They were, however, ignorant rustics and dull of understanding. . . . From this and other plagues of heresy England has certainly been free (*immunis*), although in other parts of the world so many heresies have sprouted up. There were thirty of them, both men and women, under the leadership of one Gerard, who alone was educated. In nation and language they were Teutons, but they had contrived to bewitch with their sorceries a little woman of England." Examined by the Council of Bishops summoned by the King, Gerard said they were Christians and venerated Apostolic doctrine, but rejected Holy Baptism, the Eucharist, marriage and Catholic unity. Refusing to recant, they were handed over to the secular arm, branded on the forehead, beaten, expelled out of the city and made outlaws. Only "the little woman " recanted ; the remainder perished miserably by cold and exposure.

to receive any known to be followers of that heresy."
They were to boycott them. Catholic princes were to
arrest them and confiscate their goods. Their conventicles
were to be carefully sought for, and, when discovered,
forbidden. But it is remarkable that what this " damnable heresy " consisted of is not defined, and, however
damnable, the penalties are comparatively mild—neither
prison nor death.

§ 10. COUNCIL OF LOMBERS

Whether the Tolosan authorities resented being dictated
to by a Council of Tours, or whether they connived at
the heresy they were directed to suppress, we cannot say.
But, at any rate, the Canon proved ineffective, and it was
found necessary to call another Council, and that in the
infected area itself. But it was deemed inadvisable to
summon it to meet in any of the large towns, either,
because in the quietness of a small town the business
could be transacted with greater thoroughness (cf. Nicea
in preference to Byzantium) or because the feeling
against the Church in the large centres of population
made it unsafe. Accordingly Lombers, a small town in
the Diocese of Albi, was decided upon, and here the most
important Council which had so far met, to deal with
this " damnable heresy," assembled, either in A.D. 1165
or A.D. 1176,* but the earlier date is probably correct.
Amongst those who were present were the Archbishop of
Narbonne, the Bishops of Nimes, Agde, Toulouse and
Lodève, eight Abbots, four of whom were of the Diocese
of Albi, as well as Trenveçal, Viscount of Albi, Béziers
and Carcassonne. Other princes were conspicuous by
their absence. Binius honours it with the title of " the

* For 1165 Labbe and Fleury ; also, the Archives of the Inquisition
of Carcassonne. Trenveçal, Viscount of Albi, who was present, died in
1167. For 1176 Roger de Hoveden.

Gallican Council against the Albigenses," as if all Southern France were represented ; while the official account says that its sentence was directed against those who called themselves " Boni homines."* Now, for the first time apparently, an official *inquiry* was held. The matter was not left to hearsay, but the heretics were given an opportunity to speak for themselves. Certain of their leaders, of whom Olivier was the chief, were cited to appear before the Council, and the examination was conducted by Gaucelin, Bishop of Lodève, at the instance of Gerald, Bishop of Albi. (1) They answered that they rejected the whole of the Old Testament, but accepted " the Gospels, the Epistles of Paul, the seven canonical (Catholic ?) Epistles and the Acts of the Apostles and the Apocalypse." (2) They would say nothing about their Creed unless they were forced. (3) As for the Baptism of little children, and whether they were saved, they would say nothing, but would quote from the Gospels and Epistles. (4) Questioned on the Sacrament of the Body and Blood of the Lord as to where it was consecrated, through whom they received it, and who received it, and whether the consecration was affected by the good or evil character of him who consecrated, they replied that those who received it worthily were saved, and those who received it unworthily acquired to themselves damnation, and added that it was consecrated by every good man, whether clerical or lay. Further than this they would not answer, maintaining that they ought not to be compelled to answer concerning their Creed. (5) About Matrimony they answered evasively, sheltering themselves behind a quotation from St. Paul's Epistle. (6) With regard to Penance, whether it is efficacious for salvation at the end of life, whether soldiers, mortally wounded, would be saved if they repented at the end,

* Neander, without authority, calls them Catharists.

whether each one ought to confess his sins to the priests and ministers of the Church, or to any layman whatever, or of whom St. James spake : " Confess ye your sins one to another," they said it sufficed for the weak to confess to whomsoever they would ; and as for soldiers they would say nothing, because St. James says nothing, but only about the sick. Gaucelin inquired whether, in their opinion, contrition of heart and oral confession were alone sufficient, or whether it was necessary that reparation be made after penance by fasts, scourgings, alms and lamentation for their sins, if opportunity for such presented itself. Their reply was that James said only this—that they should confess and be saved, and they did not wish to be better than the Apostle. Many things they volunteered, as that we should swear not at all, as Jesus said in the Gospel and James in his Epistle ; that Paul said in his Epistle what sort of men were to be ordained Bishops and Presbyters, and if men of other character were ordained, they were not Bishops and Presbyters, but ravening wolves and hypocrites and seducers . . . wearing white robes and gemmed rings of gold ; and therefore obedience should not be given them, since they were bad men, not good teachers, but mercenaries. The Council pronounced them guilty, and drew up a Refutation of their errors taken from the New Testament only. They retorted that the Bishop who pronounced the Sentence was himself a heretic, and turning to the people they said : " We believe "— and here they rehearsed the Articles of the Apostles' Creed, but omitting " the Holy Catholic Church." " We believe in confession of heart and mouth. We believe that he who does not eat the Body of Christ is not saved, and that it is not consecrated except in the Church, and by a priest, good or evil, and that it is not better done by a good priest than by an evil. We believe that no one is saved except by baptism, and that little children are saved by baptism. We believe that married people are saved." They further declared that they would believe anything that could be proved from the Gospels and Epistles, but that they would swear to nothing.

The result, or rather lack of results, of this Council is perplexing. Either Gaucelin was a poor examiner, or was afraid to press his examination too far. Had he been a better or a bolder examiner, he must have quickly discovered that the differentiation between the Old and the New Testaments was due to strong Dualistic tendencies. Also, this Council was the most formidable array of the powers that be which the heretics had had to face. Yet no penalties are imposed, much less inflicted upon the guilty. The Council contents itself with a mere Refutation. The most probable explanation is that the people were not overawed by the move of the Church authorities from Tours to Lombers, and the latter were not ready for an explosion. The heretics candidly avowed that their answers were *ad captandum vulgus*, " propter dilectionem et gratiam vestri," and the Council did not venture further than the mild objection : " Vos non dicitis, quod propter gratiam Domini dicatis."

§ II. A PREACHING EXPERIMENT

No help was to be expected at this time from the Pope in the suppression of heresy either in the South of France or the North of Italy, for he had more than he could manage in his struggle with Barbarossa and his Anti-pope. The Council had done little more than advertise its own weakness and the strength of the heretics. The Church therefore determined upon new methods, meeting preaching by preaching. Persuasion is better than force, but persuasion is more effective when coupled with force—

or hints of severe penalties for contumacy. The Kings of France and England sent out the Cistercian monk, Peter Chrysogonus, Cardinal and Legate, with certain Archbishops and Bishops " ut *praedicatione sua* haereticos illos ad fidem Christianam converterent," Raymond, Count of Toulouse and Raymond, Count of Castranuovo, and others lending them secular support. This move proved more successful than the Council, and many yielded. Sometimes the Commission would summon or invite the heretics to be more explicit as to their creed, granting them a safe conduct *eundi et redeundi*. Under these conditions two heresiarchs came forward, called Raymond and Bernard, and produced a certain paper in which they had drawn up the articles of their faith. But they could scarcely speak a word of Latin, and the Court " condescended " to hold the discussion in the vulgar tongue. They answered, " sane et circumspecte, ac si Christiani essent ; " so much so indeed, that they were charged with deliberate lying, and accused of holding the usual erroneous opinions with which previous investigations have made us familiar. This they strenuously denied. They even asserted their belief that " panis et vinum in corpus et sanguinem Christi vere transubstantiabantur." But to this creed they would not swear, deeming oaths unlawful. The Court regarded this avowal as a mere cloke of duplicity and condemned and excommunicated them. This sentence Peter Chrysogonus justified in an open letter, and Henry of Clairvaux, who accompanied him, in a similar letter declared that if they had deferred their visit for three years scarcely anyone would have remained orthodox.

§ 12. THIRD LATERAN COUNCIL

Alexander III, having composed his differences with Frederick Barbarossa and the Anti-pope, summoned,

in A.D. 1179, the third Lateran Council. It was described
as " A magnificent Diet of the Christian world." Over
one thousand Bishops and Abbots (amongst them
English*, Irish† and Scotch), were present, besides many
of the inferior clergy and representatives of Emperor and
Kings. By its twenty-seventh Canon it condemned the
heretics of Gascony, Albi and the parts about Toulouse,
going under several names. If they died in sin no masses
were to be said for their souls, nor were they to receive
Christian burial.‡ One incident, however, at this Council,
which received but scant notice at the time, has an
important bearing upon our subject. This was a deputa-
tion of two Waldenses who begged official recognition
of their movement from the Pope. We are concerned
here only with their doctrines, which they professed to
draw entirely from the Bible and the authoritative
utterances of the Saints (*auctoritates sanctorum*). Had
Alexander III been a Pope of statesmanlike prescience,
the Preaching Orders which eventually saved the Church
might have been anticipated by some thirty years.
These Waldenses had no certain dwelling-place, travelled
barefoot, wore woollen clothes only, had no private
property, but " had all things in common," they followed
naked the naked Christ. The Pope, to whom they
gave a book containing the text of the Psalter with notes

* Hugo, Bp. of Durham ; John, Bp. of Norwich ; Robert, Bp. of
Hereford ; and Reginald, Bp. of Bath—the maximum number invited.

† Laurence, Archbp. of Dublin, and Catholicus, Archbp. of Tuam,
and five or six bishops (Binius).

‡ Binius mentions some of their opinions, which he assigns,
erroneously, to the Waldenses. (1) No obedience to the Roman
Pontiff ; his decrees are nullius momenti. (2) Judgement by blood
forbidden. (3) Righteous laymen can consecrate : unrighteous laymen
lose their power. (4) Consecration of the elements once in the year,
without " hoc est corpus meum," but by saying Pater noster seven
times. (5) Derided indulgences, purgatory, invocation of saints,
miracles, feasts and fasts of the Church, Angel's salutation and Apostles'
creed. (6) Urenti carnis libidine omnem carnalem commixtionem
licitam esse. (7) The " Perfect " ought not to do manual labour.

and several other books of " either Law," approved of
their vow of voluntary poverty, but refused them permission to preach, unless the clergy (*sacerdotes*) asked
them. Walter Mapes, an Englishman, afterwards a
Franciscan, tells us (" De Nugis " i. 31) that he met the
Waldenses in Rome. He calls them ignorant and unlearned, and by command of the Pope entered into conversation with them, asking them at first the easiest
questions, e.g. " Did they believe in God the Father ?
and in the Son ? and in the Holy Ghost ? " To each
they answered, " We believe." " And in the Mother of
Christ ? " But when they answered again, " We believe,"
they were greeted with a general shout of laughter, and
retired in confusion, " et merito, quia a nullo regebantur
et rectores appetebant fieri, Phaetonis instar, qui nec
nomina novit equorum." The Abbot of Urspegensis, in
his Chronicle (A.D. 1212), also mentions this petition of
the Waldenses for Papal recognition, adding that they
wore capes, like the " religious," and had long hair,
unless they were " laymen." Men and women travelled
together, which caused considerable scandal. Yet they
asserted all these things came down from the Apostles.

§ 13. A PAPAL DECREE

Two years later Lucius III, on becoming Pope, issued
a decree against the heretics under various names,
including " Cathari, Patarini et ii qui se Humiliati vel
Pauperes de Lugduno falso nomine mentiuntur." They
were banned with a perpetual anathema, and were to
be destroyed by the secular arm ; but no errors are
specified.

§ 14. ALAN DE INSULIS

At the third Lateran Council was present Alan, Bishop
of Antissiodorensis, otherwise known as Alan de Insulis,

Alan the Great, Alan the Universal Doctor. He was born A.D. 1114 at Lille in Flanders, although others, e.g. Demster, identify De Insulis with Mona (Man or Anglesea). As a boy he entered Clairvaux under Bernard, and in A.D. 1151 was made a Bishop. In A.D. 1183, by command, he wrote a work in four books, dedicated to " his most beloved lord, William, by the grace of God Count of Montpelier." The title of the work is, " De Fide Catholica contra haereticos sui temporis *praesertim Albigenses*." The Albigenses, however, are not mentioned by name throughout the work. The second book is entitled, " Contra Waldenses," in which he says : " The Waldenses are so called from their heresiarch, Waldus, who, of his own will (*suo spiritu ductus*), not sent by God, started a *new* sect, presuming forsooth to preach without the authority of a Bishop, without the inspiration of God, without learning. They assert that no one should be obeyed but God only (which is explained by what he states later—that it was their opinion that obedience should be given to good prelates only and to the imitators of the Apostles). Neither office nor Order avails anything for consecrating or blessing, for binding or loosing. Where a priest is not available, confession may be made to a layman. On no account must one take an oath. On no account must a man be killed. Alan charged them with holding Docetic views of our Lord, and with declaring that the Virgin Mary was created in heaven and had no father or mother.

Bernard, the Praemonstratensian, Abbot of Fontcaud, wrote in A.D. 1190 a book " against the sect of the Waldenses," but adds nothing to our knowledge. Nor does Bonacursus, writing later in the same year, except some gross and preposterous distortion of their belief on the monthly motions of the moon, and the statement that they held that Christ was not equal to the Father.

Ten years later Ermengard wrote a tract,* also entitled "Against the sect of the Waldenses," but they
are not named in it, and those whom he attacks are not
the original or genuine Waldenses, for he charges them
with (1) Dualistic opinions ; (2) teaching that the law
of Moses was given by the Prince of evil spirits ; (3)
Docetic views ; (4) stating that in "Hoc est corpus
meum," "*hoc* does not refer to the bread which He (our
Lord) held in His hands and blessed and brake and
distributed to His disciples, but to His Body which was
performing all these things. . . . And there are some
heretics who believe that by hearing the word of God
they eat the flesh of the Son of Man and drink His blood."
He gives an interesting account of the Consolamentum,
but this will be described later.

§ 15. PETER DE VAUX-SARNAI

In the "Historia Albigensium" of the Cistercian Peter
de Vaux-Sarnai we pass from scattered references to a
work devoted specifically to their doctrines and doings.
It is dedicated to Innocent III, the Pope who passed
from words to deeds, working out a definite policy for
their absolute extinction.   The monk claims to set
down "the simple truth in a simple way," and we may
add "for simple readers," if the following description
of Raymond, Count of Toulouse, is a sample of his claim :
"A limb of the devil, a son of perdition, the first-born
of Satan, an enemy of the Cross and persecutor of the
Church, defender of heretics, suppressor of Catholics,
servant of perdition, abjurer of the Faith, full of crime,
a store-house of all sins."   Several of his statements
about their doctrines and practices lack confirmation
from any other source, especially some too blasphemous

* "Gretzer," Vol. XII.

to be repeated here. After the usual charge of the two
Gods, good and evil,* he says that they accepted only
those parts of the Old Testament which are quoted in
the New. John the Baptist was one of the greater
demons. There were two Christs—the bad one was
born in Bethlehem and crucified in Jerusalem. The
good Christ never assumed real (*veram*) flesh, and never
was in this world, except spiritually in the body of
Paul. The heretics imagined a new and invisible earth,
and there, according to some, the good Christ was born
and crucified. The good God had two wives, Colla and
Coliba, and had sons and daughters. *Others* say there
is one Creator who had as sons Christ and the Devil.
They say, too, that all the Creators were good, but that
all things were corrupted by the daughters spoken of in
the Apocalypse. Almost the whole of the Roman Church
is a den of thieves, and is "illa meretrix" mentioned in the
Apocalypse. On the Sacraments they held views already
ascribed by Eymeric to the Manichees, and mentioned
by others, "instilling into the ears of the simple this
blasphemy, that, had the body of Christ been as large as
the Alps, it would long ago have been consumed by the
partakers thereof."† "Some, denying the resurrection
of the flesh, said that our souls were those angelic spirits
which, after being thrust out of heaven through the
pride of apostasy, left their glorified bodies in the air,
and after a seven-times succession in certain terrestrial
bodies as a sort of penance returned to their own bodies
that had been left." Some are called "perfecti" or
"boni homines," others "credentes." The "perfecti"
wear black and profess (though they lie) chastity. The

---

* The first creator was (i) a liar, because he said man should surely
die if he ate of the tree, and he did not ; and (ii) a murderer because he
sent the Flood.

† Paschasius Radbert used the same argument.

"credentes" live a secular life and do not attain to the life of the "perfecti," though one with them in faith and un-faith (*fide et infidelitate*). However wickedly they have lived, yet they believe that if, "in supremo mortis articulo," they say a Pater noster and receive imposition of hands from their "masters," they will be saved ; no credent about to die can be saved without this imposition of hands. They call their masters deacons and bishops. If any "perfect" sin a mortal sin, e.g. by eating the very smallest portion of meat, egg or cheese, all who have been "consoled" by him *lose* the Holy Spirit and ought to be "consoled" again. The Waldenses also are evil, but much less so than the other heretics. "In many things they agree with us : in some disagree." They omit many of the others' infidelities. They carry sandals, and say that so long as a man carries these, if need arise, he can without episcopal ordination make (*conficere*) the Body of Christ.

§ 16. REINÉRI SACCHO

Peculiar interest attaches to the statements of Reinéri Saccho* because he had once been a Catharist (but not a Waldensian), and wrote as an Inquisitor (A.D. 1254). He distinguishes between Catharist and Waldensian, but his remarks refer primarily to the heretics of Lombardy, although he is careful to point out that their opinions differ little from Catharists in Provençe and other places. He charges the *Waldensians* with thirty-three errors, amongst which are :

(2) Belief in Traducianism. "The soul of the first man was made materially from the Holy Spirit, and the rest through it by traduction."

* "Gretzer," Vol. XII.

(6) Any good man may be a son of God in the same way as Christ was, having a soul instead of a Godhead.

(8) To adore or worship the body of Christ, or any created thing, or images or crosses, is idolatry.

(9) Final penance (*poenitentia*) avails nothing.

(11) The souls of good men enter and leave their bodies without sin.

(12) The punishment of Purgatory is nothing else than present trouble.

(14) Prayers for the dead avail nothing.

(15) Tenths and other benefactions should be given to the poor, not to the priests.

(18) They derided Church music and the Canonical Hours.

(19) Prayers in Latin profit nothing, because they are not understood.

(23) The Roman Church is not the head of the Church. It is a Church of malignants.

(31) Any man may divorce his wife and follow them, even if his wife is unwilling to be divorced, and e converso.

(33) No one can be saved outside their sect.

In addition to these he mentions other of their errors : Infant Baptism profits nothing—priests in mortal sin cannot consecrate—transubstantiation takes place in the hand, not of him who consecrates, but of him who worthily receives : consecration may be made at an ordinary table (quoting Mal. i. 11)—Mass is nothing, because the Apostles had it not—no one can be absolved by a bad priest—a good layman has power to absolve : he can also remit sins by the imposition of hands, and give the Holy Spirit—Public Penance is to be reprobated, especially in the case of women—married persons sin mortally, if they come together without hope of offspring—Holy Orders, Extreme Unction and the tonsure were derided—every one without distinction of sex may preach—Holy Scripture has the same effect in the vulgar tongue as in Latin—the Waldenses knew by heart the text of the New Testament, and a great part of the Old—they despised decretals, excommunications, absolutions, indulgences, all saints but the Apostles, canonizations, relics, crosses, times and seasons—they said in general that the doctrines of Christ and His Apostles were sufficient for salvation without the statutes of the Church.

With regard to the Catharists he observed that they were divided into three divisions—Albanenses, Concorezenses and Bognolenses. There were others in Tuscany, the Marquisate of Treves and in *Provence* who differed very little, if at all, from those previously mentioned. The opinions *common* to them all were :

(1) The Devil made the world and all things in it.

(2) All the Sacraments of the Church are of the Devil, and the Church itself is a Church of malignants.

(3) Carnal marriage is always a mortal sin.

(4) There is no resurrection of the flesh.

(5) It is mortal sin to eat eggs, flesh and such-like.

(6) It is mortal sin for the secular power to punish heretics or malefactors.

(7) There is no such thing as Purgatory.

(8) Whoever kills an animal commits a great sin.

(9) They had four Sacraments : (*a*) Imposition of hands, called Consolamentum, but by that imposition of hands and the saying of the Lord's Prayer there is no remission of sins if the person officiating be in mortal sin ; (*b*) Benediction of the Bread ; (*c*) Penance ; (*d*) Orders.

To the Catharists of Toulouse he ascribes the following

doctrines (which they held in common with the Albanenses) :

(10) There are two principles, Good and Evil.

(11) There is no Trinity in the Catholic sense, for the
Father is greater than the Son and the Holy Ghost.

(12) The world and all that is in it were created by the
evil God.

(13) They held some Valentinian ideas.

(14) The Son of Man was not really incarnate in the
Virgin Mary, and did not eat—in short, Docetism.

(15) The patriarchs were the servants of the Devil.

(16) The Devil was the author of the Old Testament,
except Job, Psalms, Proverbs, Wisdom, Ecclesiasticus
and the Major and Minor Prophets.

(17) The world will never end.

(18) The Judgement is past.

(19) Hell is in this world.

This detailed examination of the heresy is of great
importance, not only on account of the peculiar ad-
vantages which Reinéri Saccho possessed as both heretic
and inquisitor, but because it shews that even at this
late stage, Catharist and Waldensian had not been
welded into one under the blows of a persecution directed
equally against both. At one in their hatred of the
Roman Church and all its works, there is a marked
difference in their deism. The Waldensian, according
to Saccho's classification, knows nothing of Dualism, is
sound on the doctrine of the Trinity, and believes both
Old and New Testaments to be the Word of God. The
Catharist, on the other hand, believes in a good and an
evil God, the latter being the Creator of the world of
matter, which therefore is itself evil. Hence, whatever
perpetuates matter, e.g. marriage, is also evil ; but the
world being the work of a God must also, like its maker,

be endless. That part of the Old Testament which describes its beginning and its development into kingdoms and hierarchies, together with all their chief representatives, be they patriarchs, princes or priests, has the evil God for its author. Only the poets and the prophets who took a more spiritual view of things earthly, are inspired by the good God.

§ 17. INQUISITIONS

By the middle of the thirteenth century the coercive measures which Rome took for the suppression of heresy had proved successful. No longer was there any need for Councils to examine and pass judgment upon it, nor defenders of the faith to write against it. It had become *une chose jugée.* Henceforth the Church dealt with individuals, and by means of ecclesiastical Courts, called the Inquisition, arrested, questioned and decided whether a person, charged with heresy, was guilty or not. Unfortunately for the cause of history the earlier records, or Acta, of these Inquisitions were, in their brief spells of resurgence, destroyed by the Catharists and Waldenses, as containing dangerous evidence against them. Only the later ones have survived. Limborch, who made the Inquisition his special study, published the " Book of the Sentences " which the Inquisition of Toulouse (A.D. 1300) pronounced against the Waldenses and Albigenses, and he came to the conclusion that while they had some dogmas in common, they had different opinions and were separate sects. According to him the Waldenses and Albigenses had only three opinions in common : (1) All oaths are unlawful ; (2) any good man can receive a Confession, but only God can absolve from sin ; (3) no obedience is due to the Roman Church. The following opinions he ascribes to the Albigenses, and not to the Waldenses : (1) There are two Gods, good and evil ;

(2) the Sacraments of the Church of Rome are vain and unprofitable—the Eucharist is merely bread—a man is saved by the imposition of their hands—sins are remitted without Confession and satisfaction— Baptism avails nothing ; Baptism by water is of no benefit to children, since they are so far from consenting to it that they weep—the Order of St. James, or Extreme Unction, made by material oil, signifies nothing ; they prefer imposition of hands—repudiate the constitution of the whole Roman Church, and deny to all the Prelates of it the power of binding and loosing, on the ground that they are greater sinners than those whom they claim to bind and loose ; but they (the Albigenses) can give the Holy Spirit—matrimony is always sinful, except spiritual matrimony ; (3) Christ did not take a real human body, but only the likeness of one—the Virgin Mary is not and was not a real woman ; the Virgin Mary is true penitence whereby people are born into their Church ; (4) there is a kind of spiritual body or inner man whereby persons rise from the dead ; (5) the Cross is the sign of the Devil, and should not be adored, since no man adores the gallows on which his father was hanged ; (6) souls are spirits banished from heaven on account of their sins ; (7) they deny purgatory altogether.

Opinions ascribed to the Waldenses, but not to the Albigenses : (1) all judgement is forbidden of God, and therefore it is a sin for any judge to condemn a man to any punishment (St. Matt. vii.) ; (2) indulgences are worthless ; (3) purgatory exists only in this life, and therefore prayers cannot profit the dead ; (4) the Church has only three Orders—Bishops, Priests and Deacons ; (5) laymen can preach ; (6) matrimony is sinful only when people marry without hope of offspring.

The Records of the several Inquisitions are helpful in

the particulars which they furnish of the government, organization and services of the Albigenses and Waldenses. Unfortunately in many cases their dates and places are missing, and hence they fail us in an attempt to trace any change or development in their doctrines. The general date of these Acta is the beginning of the fourteenth century, and from these and certain scraps of other Inquisitions which have been preserved, we are able to amplify somewhat Limborch's conclusions. Thus the Report of the Inquisition of Carcassonne treats separately "De Manichaeis moderni temporis" and "De Waldensibus moderni temporis," whose origin they trace to a certain citizen of Lyons, Valdesius or Valdens, in A.D. 1170, and who spread to Lombardy, "et praecisi ab ecclesia, cum aliis haereticis se miscentes et eorum errores imbibentes, suis adinventionibus antiquorum haereticorum errores et haereses miscuerunt." As the Report adds "quia olim plures alios habuerunt," we cannot say whether in the opinion of the Court the balance was or was not in favour of the Waldenses, but it does mark a change, by subtraction and addition, in the total. The Inquisitors complained that the Waldenses were very slippery and evasive under examination. When driven into a corner, they would plead that they were unlearned, simple folk and did not understand the question. Then they contended that to take an oath was a clear violation of Christ's words in St. Matthew v., and therefore a grievous sin ; yet according to the Report of the Inquisition of Carcassonne they pleaded that they might swear if by so doing they could escape death themselves or screen others from death by not betraying their friends or revealing the secrets of their sect. Their defence was that they were filled with the Holy Ghost and were doing His work ; to injure or cut short that work was to sin the sin against the Holy

Ghost, which hath never forgiveness. Thus in a law-suit a heretic might take the oath, because refusal meant revelation ; he would be absolved on confession. But when they were ordered to take the oath, " juro per ista sancta evangelia quod nunquam didici vel credidi aliquid quod sit contra fidem veram quam sancta Romana ecclesia credit et tenet," with uplifted hand and touching the Gospels, i.e. ex animo, they prevaricated. Another instance of this evasiveness was their outward conformity to the established religion. They would attend Church and behave with the utmost decorum ; in conversation with a known Catholic their speech was most orthodox and prudent. Although they would not touch a woman, or even sit on the same bench with her, however great the distance between them, they travelled with them, because it would be then supposed that they were their wives, and hence that they themselves were not heretics. They denied that prayers *of* saints or *to* saints were of any avail, yet they abstained from work on Saints' Days, unless they could work unobserved. A " Perfect " must not be married, but if he burn, he could satisfy the lust of the *flesh* so long as he remained pure in *heart*. This concession they, however, kept secret from the Credents, lest they should fall in their esteem. In another Inquisition at Carcassonne, held in A.D. 1308 and 1309, " contra Albigenses," Peter and James Autéri, who with other members of their family, were the last leaders of the Albigenses, declared that true Matrimony is not between male and female, for that is two kinds of flesh, not one, whereas God said, " They two shall become *one* flesh." The true Matrimony is between the soul and the Spirit. " For in Paradise there was never a corruption of the flesh nor anything which was not simply (*merum*) and purely spiritual, and God made Matrimony itself for this end—that souls which had fallen from Heaven through pride in ignorance and were in this world should return to life by (*cum*) the Matrimony of the Holy Spirit, viz. by good works and abstinence from sins, and ' they two would become one flesh ' (*in carne una*)."*

The testimony of Raymond de Costa given before the Inquisition of Languedoc is so divergent from all other evidence and so subversive of the fundamental principles and practices of the Waldenses that, although he was a Waldensian Deacon, his statements may be received with suspicion. According to him the Credents were instructed to obey the Curés of the Roman Church and to attend Mass because there they could see the Body of Jesus Christ and adore it (or Him), and pray for a good end and forgiveness of sins. Their Sacraments and those of the Roman Church were equally valid. Peter was the head of the Church after Christ, and the Roman Pontiffs after Peter, and their own " Majors " were under the Pope ; if the Roman Church disappeared, they would all become pagans. The chief points on which their " Majors " differed from the Roman Church were Purgatory and Oaths, and the Church would grievously sin if it excommunicated him for not swearing, or for not believing that Purgatory was in the other world. Under further examination, and with time for reflection, he revoked some of his former opinions, from which we may perhaps conclude they were his own rather than Waldensian. Thus, at the first examination he maintained that, in face of St. John iii., not even a martyr was saved if he had not been baptized with

---

* This view of carnal Matrimony being a sin is also given in a book called " Supra Stella," by Salve Burce, a citizen of Piacenza, A.D. 1235, in which all heretics are charged with agreeing that " Matrimony makes us debtors to the flesh," which saints must not be (Rom. viii). Frederick William Garsias declared before the Inquisition of Carcassonne that there was no Matrimony except between the soul and God.

water, but this he afterwards withdrew, as also the statement that no one who was married could be ordained in their sect ; but he would swear to neither.*

We have seen that the heretics believed in the absolute sanctity of human life, and declared that not even a judge had power to condemn any man to death. If the positions were reversed, and they were the stronger party, they would not put to death even the most obstinate Catholic. Yet this was only theory, and often yielded under a necessity which knows no law. Thus Raymond Valsiera of Ax, a " Manichee," declared that he had been taught by William Autéri that it was wrong to kill either man or animal ; nevertheless, he ought to kill a Catholic who persecuted them ; and as a matter of fact, Raymond Issaura acknowledged to the Inquisition of Carcassonne " against the Albigenses," A.D. 1308, that his brother, William, with three others, had waylaid a Beguin who confessed that he had been plotting the capture of Peter and William Autéri, and that they had killed him and thrown his body into a crevasse. And on the question of revenge generally, the theory of its sinfulness was argued differently by Catharists and Waldenses, according to the Book called " Supra Stella."† The Waldenses maintained that revenge was allowed by God in Old Testament times, but the Catharists maintained that that God was the evil God. Both parties appealed to Christ's words in St. Matt. v. 38, " Ye have heard that it was said by them of old time . . . but I say unto you," the Waldenses arguing that Jesus accepted revenge as permissible under the Old Covenant, and the Catharists

* It is worth while noticing that this withdrawal was made when it was pointed out to him that the *Eastern Church* did not enforce celibacy on its clergy. Does this show a lingering preference for the East as against the West ?

† *v.* p. 60, note.

that Jesus knew that that law originated from the evil God and therefore substituted another. The same arguments were used by each with regard to oaths.

When once the persecutions had got the heretics " on the run," they found it difficult not only to maintain their interdenominational union, but also denominational unity of doctrine. Differences manifest themselves amongst the scattered groups of the Waldenses themselves. Thus those who are described as " the heresiarchs of Lombardy," probably to be identified with those Waldenses who had mixed themselves with other heretics there,* sent a Rescript to the Leonists (i.e. Poor Men of Lyons) in Germany, informing them of the points of controversy between themselves and those whom they called " Ultramontanos dictos Valdesii socios," i.e. those who had remained in Southern France. It states that the chief point of difference is on the Sacraments. The Ultramontane Waldenses did not believe anyone could be saved unless he were baptized with water. Marriage could not be dissolved, except by consent of both parties, or on some ground which commended itself to the community. They held that Peter Waldo was in the Paradise of God, and they could have no communion with any who denied it. With regard to the Holy Communion they maintained that " the substance of the bread and wine is changed into the Body and Blood of Christ by the sole utterance (*prolatio*) of the Lord's words,"† adding : " We attribute the virtue not to man, but to the words of God ; " to which those of Lombardy objected : " Anyone, whether Jew or Gentile, by uttering these words may make (*conficiat*) the Body and Blood of Christ." They carried their objection

---

* *v.* p. 58. Had they been Cathari, the points of controversy would have been more pronounced and fundamental.

† *v.* p. 63.

further, because the Ultramontane associates of Waldesius " held that no one could baptize who could not make (*valet conficere*) the Body of Christ ; " and as it was agreed that *anyone* might baptize, it would follow that anyone could consecrate, whether layman or laywoman, however wicked. But the Ultramontanes guarded themselves against this inference by laying it down that the Breaking of the Bread could only be done by a presbyter ; and further that the actual change (*transubstantiatur*) of the substance of the visible bread and wine is made by neither a good man nor a bad man, but only by Him who is God and Man, i.e. by Christ. In that view the Lombards agreed, but disagreed in the opinion that the prayer of an adulterer or any other evildoer was heard by God in that Sacrament. The fact of transubstantiation depended upon valid ordination of the minister and upon God hearing his prayer. When these two essentials are present, then after benediction transubstantiation takes place. If the minister himself is reprobate, his prayer affects adversely himself only, and not the worthy communicant.

A religion which claims the faith and obedience of man is bound to offer to man some explanation of his nature, or in other words, of that dualism of good and evil of which every man is conscious. The early Christian Fathers, as against the Dualistic theology of the Gnostics —a good and evil god—and consequently a Dualistic anthropology—the good soul and the evil flesh—drew a distinction between the צֶלֶם and the דְּמוּת, or the εἰκών and the ὁμοίωσις of the one God in which that one God created man—the " image " being that which man essentially is, and the " likeness " that to which he arrives by a right use of his original capacities. The heretics, while presenting a creed fundamentally Dualistic, either absolute or mitigated, did not at first address

themselves to this question of the origin of evil in man,
but merely assumed it ; but it was not a point that
could be shelved. With some variations the solution was
at length propounded that the good God had created
only a limited number of good spirits,* but that the
evil god (or *Satanael*,† a fallen angel) introduced to these
good spirits a beautiful woman by whom they were
seduced from their allegiance to the good God.   These
fallen spirits the evil god provided with tunics, i.e.
bodies of flesh, so that they might forget their first
estate. Death was the passing of the spirit from tunic
to tunic, i.e. from one body to another, until it came
into that tunic in which it would be saved, viz. as a
believer in their (the heretics') faith, and so return in
that tunic to heaven. This was the testimony of James
Autéri, one of that famous family who did so much to
fan into flame the dying embers of Catharism at the
beginning of the fourteenth century.   Another (un-
named) witness declared that when the Son of God
came down from heaven, 144,000 angels came with
Him, and they remained in the world to receive the
souls of those who obeyed God, i.e. heretics, and carry
them back to heaven.

* This was also the opinion of Origen.
† Or the Satan-God.

CHAPTER IV

THE SYSTEM

(A) CONSTITUTION AND ORDERS

§ I. ATTITUDE TO ROMAN CATHOLICISM

A MOVEMENT which claimed to be a revival, and even a survival, of primitive Christianity would not be likely to frame its constitution and orders upon the lines of a Church which it regarded as hopelessly corrupt, and which subjected it to pitiless persecution ; any likeness between the two would be due merely to the claim or fact that they were derived from a common source. The Roman Church had three Orders—Priests, Deacons, and Sub-deacons ; the Catharists also had three Orders—Majors, Presbyters and Deacons ; but the difference was fundamental, for whereas the Roman Orders were sacramental, the Catharist were merely executive. Apostolic Succession was not confined to commissioned officers, but included the rank and file. It was proved not by ecclesiastical pedigrees, but by personal experience and responsive conduct. For it was the direct gift of the Holy Spirit to the individual, and was not mediated through man. These Spirit-filled persons composed the true Church. It is less true to say that the heretics were " praecisi ab ecclesia "* than that they deliberately repudiated and left the Church because it had forfeited its status by quenching the Holy Spirit,

---

* Inquis. of Carcassonne " De Manichaeis moderni temporis " (p. 58).

as was shewn by its corruptions and persecutions. The loss of the Holy Spirit involved the loss of its power to excommunicate. Only those were successors of the Apostles who copied their life.

As life is in the whole body and in every member of the body, so the Holy Spirit was in their Church and in every member of the same. Hence, too, every local Church possessed the authority of the whole to elect its officers, whose authority, again, was not limited to such local Church, but could be exercised anywhere. Nor, when once conferred, was this authority regarded as a personal charisma. They did not say : " Ego te absolvo," but " Deus tua peccata tibi dimittat."*

The Waldenses, however, were less uncompromising in their attitude towards Roman Orders. Thus Raymond, the Waldensian Deacon, in his inquisition at Languedoc, declared that their Majors did *not* have the keys of the kingdom of heaven, but did have the *same* powers of Absolution as Bishops of the Roman Church, and that their Presbyters had equal powers with the priests of the Roman Church, " quia idem sunt in fide et in credulitate." On the other hand, Raymond Valsiera of Ax, described as a Manichee, and a pupil of the intransigeant William Autéri, in his confession, denied to the prelates and priests of the Roman Church any power to absolve, because they were the enemies of the Holy Faith.

§ 2. CREDENTS

Adherents were divided into Credents and Perfects, the latter being the more advanced. A movement exposed to constant persecution and espionage would exercise the greatest care in admission to its membership, and only after the most searching examination and most

* Inquis. of Languedoc, beginning of fourteenth century (Cod. Vat. 4070).

solemn promises were its doors thrown open to applicants. Initiation into membership was called by enemies "heretication," and was of a more elaborate character with the Catharists than with the Waldenses. According to Peter de Vaux-Sarnai in his "Historia Albigensium," the Waldenses, of whom he held a higher opinion than of other heretics,[*] had an initiatory rite which involved a total renunciation of their Roman baptism and Creed. "When any one joins the heretics, he who receives him says, 'Friend, if you wish to be of us, you ought to renounce the whole Faith which the Roman Church holds.' He answers, 'I do renounce it.' 'Therefore receive the Holy Spirit from good men,' and then he breathes seven times on his face. Then he says to him, 'Do you renounce that cross which the priest made on you in your baptism on breast and shoulders and head with oil and chrism?' He answers, 'I do renounce it.' 'Do you believe that water works salvation for you?' He answers, 'I do not believe it.' 'Do you renounce that veil which the priest placed on your head for you when you were baptized?' He answers, 'I do renounce it.' Then he receives the baptism of the heretics. All then place their hands upon his head and kiss him and clothe him in a black robe, and from that hour he is one of them." This catechism confirms the statement of Ermengard, who wrote a tract against the Waldenses (although he does not mention them by name) that the sacrament of Baptism was unprofitable, unless a person answered with his own mouth and from his heart. Imposition of hands was substituted for affusion of water, the kiss of peace for the oil of chrism, so that the charge of *Ana*baptism cannot be maintained.

We are better served in our information of Catharist

---

[*] "Quidem mali erant, sed comparatione aliorum haereticorum *longe minus perversi.*"

ritual since the publication by L. Cledat in 1887 of the New Testament,* which was translated in the thirteenth century into Provençal, and to which is appended the Catharist ritual preserved in folio 235 of MS. 36 of the MSS. in the Library of St. Peter's Palace at Lyons.

The Credents had first of all to make their confession in these words : " We confess our sins before God and you, and before the ordinances of Holy Church, that we may receive pardon and penance for all sins in thought and word and deed, and for all offences in the sight of the Father, the Son and the honoured Holy Spirit and of the honoured holy Apostles, by prayer and faith and by the salvation of all the loyal glorious Christians and blessed ancestors asleep and the brethren here present, and before you, holy Lord, that you may pardon all that in which we have sinned. Benedicite, parcite nobis. And whereas the holy word of God instructs us, as also the holy Apostles, and our spiritual brethren tell us that we should renounce all the lusts of the flesh and all impurity, we confess that we have not done so. Benedicite, parcite nobis." (Other sins are also confessed, and each confession ends with " Benedicite, parcite nobis ").

" The Credent must then fast, and when the Christians agree to deliver to him the orison (Lord's Prayer) they shall wash their hands, and the Credent shall do likewise. Then one of the Good Men, who is next unto the Elder, shall make three bows (*révérances*) to the Elder, and then prepare a table, and having made three more

* M. Chabaneau (" Revue des langues romanes," XXXIII, 462) remarks that several of the passages quoted in the ritual from the N.T. as well as the ritual itself present features characteristic of the dialect in Vaudois books, a fact which, he points out, should not be overlooked in considering the problem, " qu'on croit peut-être à tort pleinement résolu," of the origin of the ritual of Lyons.

bows, shall place a cloth upon it, and having made three more bows, shall place the book upon the cloth, and shall say, ' Benedicite, parcite nobis.' Then the Credent shall make his melioramentum,* and take the book from the hand of the Elder, who shall then admonish him and preach to him with suitable proofs (*témoignages*). And if the Credent is called Peter, he shall say : ' Peter, you must understand that you are before the Church of God, you are before the Father, the Son and the Holy Spirit. For the Church means union, and where are true Christians, there are the Father, Son and Holy Spirit (St. Matt. xviii. 20 ; St. John xiv. 23 ; 2 Cor. vi. 16, 18 ; xiii. 2 ; 1 Tim. iii. 14, 15 ; Heb. iii. 6). The Spirit of God is with the faithful of Jesus Christ, and Christ dwells in them [as stated] in St. John xiv. 15–18 ; St. Matt. xxviii. 20 ; 1 Cor. iii. 16, 17 ; St. Matt. x. 20 ; 1 St. John iv. 13 ; Gal. iv. 6. For God's people separated themselves of old from their Lord God. And they separated themselves from the counsel and will of their Holy Father by the deceit of evil spirits and by yielding to their will. And for these and many other reasons they were made to understand that the Holy Father wishes to have mercy upon His people, and to receive them into peace and concord by the advent of His Son, Jesus Christ, and this is your opportunity. For you are here before the disciples of Jesus Christ in the place where spiritually dwell the Father, the Son and the Holy Spirit, as we have shewn above, to receive the holy orison which Jesus Christ has given to His disciples in order that your orisons and prayers may be granted by our Holy Father. This is why you ought to understand, if you wish to receive this holy orison, that you must repent of all your sins and forgive all people. (St. Matt. vi. 15) . . . It follows that you purpose to

* *vide infra*, p. 84.

keep this holy orison all your life, if God give you grace
to receive it, according to the custom of the Church of
God, with chastity and truth and all other virtues which
God shall please to give you. This is why we pray to
the good Lord Who has given to the disciples of Jesus
Christ the virtue to receive this holy orison with stedfastness, that He may give you also the grace to receive
it with stedfastness, both to His honour and your salvation. P.N.'

"Then the Elder says the orison, and the Credent repeats
it. Then the Elder says : ' We deliver this holy orison
in order that you may receive it of God and of us and of
the Church, and have power to say it all your life, day
and night, alone and in company, and that you never
eat or drink without first saying this orison.' And he
shall say, ' I receive it of God and of you and of the
Church.' He shall then make his melioramentum and
give thanks, and then the Christians shall make a ' double
avec veniae ' (? ' Benedicite, parcite nobis,' twice), and
the Credent shall say it after them.

And if he ought to be ' consoled '* on the spot, the
Credent must make his melioramentum, and take the
book from the hand of the Elder. And the Elder shall
admonish him and preach to him with suitable proofs
and such words as are appropriate to his consolamentum,*
and say thus : ' Peter, you wish to receive spiritual
baptism whereby is given the Holy Spirit unto the
Church of God, with the holy orison, with the imposition
of the hands of the Good Men. Of this baptism our
Lord speaks (St. Matt. xxviii. 19, 20 ; St. Mark xvi. 15 ;
St. John iii. 5 ; i. 16, 17 ; St. Mark iii. 11 ; Acts i. 5).
This baptism by the imposition of hands has been instituted by Jesus Christ (St. Mark xvi. 18 ; Acts ix. 17, 18),
and afterwards Paul and Barnabas practised it in several

* *vide infra*, pp. 73, 83.

places. This holy baptism by which the Holy Spirit is given the Church has kept since the Apostles until now, and it has come from the Good Men to the Good Men until now, and will be unto the end of the world. And you must understand that power is given to the Church of God to bind and loose, to forgive and retain sin, as Christ said (St. John xx. 21 ; St. Matt. xvi. 18, 19 ; xviii. 19, 20 [18, 19] ; x. 8 ; St. John xiv. 12 ; St. Mark xii. 17 ; St. Luke x. 19). And if you wish to receive this power, you must keep all the commandments of Christ and the New Testament according to your power. And know that He has commanded that man shall not commit adultery, or murder, or lie ; that he shall not swear any oath ; that he shall not seize or rob ; he must pardon and love his enemies ; pray for his calumniators ; if one strike him on one cheek, turn to him the other also ; must hate the world and the things that are in the world (1 St. John ii. 16, 17 ; St. John vii. 7 ; Book of Solomon [Eccles.] i. 14 ; St. Jude, brother of St. James, 23).' And he shall say : ' I have this will : pray to God for me that He will give me His power.' And then one of the Good Men shall make his melioramentum with the Credent to the Elder and say, ' Parcite nobis. Good Christians ! we pray you by the love of God that you grant this blessing, which God has given you, to our friend here present.' And the Credent shall make his melioramentum and say, ' Parcite nobis. For all sins I ask the pardon of God and the Church and you all.' And the Christians shall say, ' By God and us and the Church they have been forgiven you. And we pray God that He will forgive you.' And then they shall console him. And the Elder shall take the book and place it upon his head and the other Good Men shall each take his right hand, and say the ' parcias ' and ' adoremus ' three times, and then : ' Holy Father, receive Thy servant into Thy righteousness and put Thy grace and holy spirit upon him.' And then they shall pray to God with the orison, and he who directs the service ought to say in a low voice the ' sixaine,' and then the ' adoremus ' three times and the orison once in a loud voice, and then the Gospel. And when the Gospel is said, they ought to say ' Adoremus ' three times and the Gratia and the Parcias."

Before a Credent was admitted to membership he had solemnly to promise to submit to the " Abstinence " or discipline of the Church which comprised certain rules of conduct, and the Church had to satisfy itself that the applicant was of sufficient moral strength to discharge his obligations. Thus, if a Christian comes into a place of danger he shall pray the Gratia. If anyone mounts a horse he shall observe the double (i.e. says the orison twice). If he goes on board ship, or enters a town, or passes over a plank or a dangerous bridge, he shall say the orison. If he finds anything on the road, he must not touch it, if he knows the owner. If he knows the owner, but cannot overtake him, he must leave the article on the road. If he wishes to drink or eat he must say the orison twice before and twice after doing so. Christians must visit sick Christians, and inquire into their life. Christians must pay their debts, and shall not be received into membership until they have done so, but if they cannot pay, they are not to be repelled on that account. They must promise to hold their heart and their goods, both present and future, at the disposal of God and the Church. If an applicant for membership agrees to all this, the Good Men answer : " We impose on you this Abstinence that you may receive it of God and of us and of the Church, and may you keep it all your life. For if you observe it well, with the other things which you have to do, we have hope that your soul will have

life." And he shall answer : " I receive it of God and
of you and of the Church."

The rite of initiation was called Consolamentum, but
further consideration of this word must be deferred
owing to certain obscurities in its use. It is sufficient
here to remark that the ceremonies accompanying it
varied according to the physical condition and ecclesiastical position of the recipient. From the chief act
in the ceremony it received the alternate title of the
imposition of hands, whereby was conveyed the gift of
the Holy Spirit the Consolator (hence its name), but the
gift could not be conveyed if the officiating minister
were in sin as interpreted by their own laws.

§ 3. PERFECTS

Next to the Credents came the Perfecti,* who undoubtedly formed the core of the whole movement.
Between the Credents and the Perfect, Peter de Vaux-
Sarnai draws the distinction as follows : " Credents are
those who love a secular life, and do not aim at imitating
the life of the Perfect, although they hope to be saved
by the same Faith. They are different in their manner of
living, but are one in faith and unfaith (*fide et infidelitate*)."
Only after a long probation and distinguished service
were they chosen to the honourable position of the
Perfect. Although, as such, the position carried with it
no special office, yet they were required to devote their
whole time to discreet propaganda and the interests of
their co-religionists. They professed absolute poverty
and were forbidden to work or to engage in any trade,
as that would expose them to lying, fraud or taking an

---

* A title based on St. Matt. xix. 21. Outside Scripture the title
meets us as early as the Council of Ancyra (A.D. 314), which is note-
worthy in view of the association of Catharism with Galatia, of which
Ancyra was the capital ; several of its Canons also deal with matters
closely resembling the doctrines and practices of the Catharists.

oath. They were supported in money, food and hospitality by the Credents. Only to avoid detection and arrest were they allowed to work; or when safe, as a protest against Catholicism on the fast days of the Church. Since from them alone were elected the officers—Majors, Elders, Deacons—it was of the utmost importance that they should observe all dietary rules as described already, since a violation of them would invalidate any ceremonial function in which they took part, e.g. the Consolamentum.* Their relation to women is not quite clear, and qualifications for " Perfection " varied. While strict celibacy was aimed at, facts modified the ideal. Some insisted that no Perfect could be married, and if married, he must dismiss his wife. Raymond de Costa, a Waldensian Deacon, affirmed that according to the New Testament, no one who had a wife could be ordained a Bishop or an Elder, and any ordination of the married was null and void. 1 Timothy iii. and Titus i. he referred to the one Church. A Perfect would not sit on the same bench with a woman, however long it might be. On the other hand, women travelled about with them to attend to their personal wants, a practice which provoked much unfavourable comment. Some excluded even widowers from the rank of Perfect. There were two grades among the Perfect—the Novellani, or novices, and the Sandaliati. These latter were promoted to the higher grade only after long and faithful and distinguished service, and for their proved knowledge of the Scriptures and ability to teach others. They dressed in black and wore sandals which protected only the soles, leaving the

---

* Si quis de perfectis peccaret mortaliter comedendo, videlicet modicissimum carnium, etc., omnes consolati ab illo amittebant Spiritum Sanctum, et oportebat eum iterum reconsolari (Peter de Vaux-Sarnai, Ermengard, etc.). But, on the other hand, as eating flesh was distasteful to them, they might eat it on Fast Days to afflict the soul, thus reversing Catholic usage (Inquis. of Carcassonne).

rest of the foot bare.* They went from place to place, encouraging the " faithful," and instructing them in the Scriptures, so far as they accepted them, and taking with them interpreters when necessary.

From the Perfect were taken the three Orders— Deacons, Presbyters (or Elders) and Majors (or Bishops†), whose authority was derived not from the Roman Church, but from the Holy Spirit in their own Church.

§ 4. DEACONS

The qualifications for the office of Deacon were membership of at least six years, a knowledge of the Scriptures, ability to say the Pater noster and Ave Maria (!),‡ a blameless life and unimpeachable loyalty, not under twenty years of age and unmarried ; if married, he was not allowed to dismiss his wife in order to be ordained. He had to take the threefold vow of chastity, poverty and obedience to Majors or Bishops. His duties were to attend upon the Majors or Bishops, as Mark upon Barnabas and Paul, when itinerating. He might be sent from one Church to another to widen his knowledge. Thus Raymond the Waldensian said, under examination, that he had been a Deacon for twenty-seven years, having been ordained by John Lotaringa, who after two years' instruction sent him to other members of the community, and he did not return for seven years. A Deacon was ordained by the prayer and imposition of the hands of a Major only, and was subject to his

* De Paup. de Lugdano (Cod. Vatic. lat. 2648, no date or author).

† Reinéri Saccho, a Catharist, not a Waldensian, gives *four* Orders. (1) Episcopus ; (2) Filius Major ; (3) Filius Minor ; (4) Diaconus (Gretzer, Vol. XII).

‡ Others deny this on the ground that it was the custom of the Roman Church. If used at all, its use was probably understood as referring to their own pure (Catharist) Church. The Waldenses did not use either the Ave Maria or the Creed.

authority. He was not allowed to hear Confessions* or to carry the reserved Sacrament or to preach, but he could read the Gospel in Church, although he seldom did so, and take a minor part with Presbyters and Majors in the election and ordination of a Major.

§ 5. PRESBYTERS

Although it is correct to speak of three orders, it does not appear that the Diaconate was that from which alone the Presbyterate was supplied. A Deacon might be " perpetual," and a Presbyter was elected direct from the ranks of the Perfect. The consent of the local Church must be unanimous. The ordination took place once or twice a year at the Conferences† at which all the business was transacted. He took the three vows of poverty, chastity and obedience. The congregation said the Lord's Prayer and confessed their sins, after which the Major and Presbyters laid their hands upon him. The only difference between the ordination of a Deacon and that of a Presbyter appears to have been that at the former the people also laid their hands upon him. A Presbyter was now qualified to hear Confessions, and impose but not remit penalties, the latter office of remission being reserved for the Major. In the absence of the Major he could " make the Body of Christ." If there was danger of the Succession failing, a Presbyter could appoint and ordain a Major, since by virtue of his forsaking all and following Christ he was like the Apostles and had Apostolic authority. As a rule, however, he only took part with other Presbyters and Deacons in the ordination of Majors. With the Waldenses the

* Inquis. of Languedoc, fourteenth century. But Reinéri Saccho, the ex-Catharist, says that the Deacons could hear confessions of venial sins once a month.
† At these Conferences no Credent, *young* Perfect or woman attended.

Clergy of the Roman Church were not " re-ordained,"
but ordered to take the above threefold vow and reminded
of the persecutions to which they were exposed, before
being allowed to officiate.

§ 6. MAJORS OR BISHOPS

This was the highest of the three Orders, although
we find traces of a superior Major, called the Pontifical, whose relation to a Major would correspond
roughly to that of an Archbishop to a Bishop. Reinéri
Saccho states that the Cathari had four Orders :
(1) Episcopus ; (2) Filius Major ; (3) Filius Minor ;
(4) Diaconus, and that on the death of a Bishop, a Filius
Minor ordained a Filius Major to be the new Bishop,
and that he in turn ordained the Filius Minor to be a
Filius Major. But some objected to this procedure on
the ground that it was like a son appointing a father.
Hence, authority was given to a Bishop to appoint
an elder son as Bishop to succeed him on his decease.
But this was not general. As a rule, as already stated,
the threefold order obtained, although possibly the
title of *Major* was taken from that of the Filius *Major*
and made equivalent to that of Episcopus. When a
vacancy in the Majoralty occurred, the Presbyters and
Deacons met together, and the oldest in orders, " like
Peter at the election of Matthias," explained the purpose of their assembly, and nominated a Presbyter for
the vacant office. His nominee then left the room, and
the president enumerated the qualifications of a Major—
learning, loyalty, length of service, personal sanctity and
capacity to rule the household, the Church, and declared
that in his opinion the Presbyter nominated possessed
all these qualifications. If the meeting agreed,* the

* Their opinions were ascertained individually, beginning with the
eldest.

Presbyter was called in, and on being questioned promised to keep the laws of the Society and to exact the obedience of all under his authority. A Major took no part in the *election* of a Major, but except in an emergency, his presence was essential to a Major's ordination. After the promise (not oath) of obedience had been given, the congregation knelt and said the Lord's Prayer ; and on rising from their knees, the Major-elect made his private confession to the Major, and a general confession to the congregation, and prayed to God to give him His Holy Spirit. Then came the most important ceremony of all, the imposition of hands, first by the Major, having obtained the assent of the congregation, and then by the Presbyters and Deacons. If, however, there was no Major present, the eldest Presbyter, with the consent of the other Presbyters and Deacons could act for him.

Neither Deacon, Presbyter nor Major wore any dress distinctive of their order. Of the Majors it was said : " He is clothed in good work, fastings and prayers ; his mitre is spiritual, i.e. his authority to rule is from God and man ; his pastoral staff also is spiritual, viz. the threatenings of Holy Scripture against sinners, and his encouragements of the weaker brethren by word and deed ; his episcopal ring was his integrity in the Faith."

The first Pontifical Major was ordained in the same way as a Major, but afterwards only a Pontifical could ordain a Pontifical. If, however, there was no Pontifical available, either by death or absence, the authority to ordain reverted to the Presbyters and Deacons.

Full disciplinary powers were vested in a Major, and therefore there could not be two Majors in one local Church. In the discipline of Deacons, he was not bound to consult the Church ; for the Deacon vowed direct obedience to the Major, and therefore the Major could inflict and remove penalties for offences. He could expel a Deacon from the Church and re-admit him. The rite for reconciliation of a Deacon was imposition of hands, but this did not imply re-ordination. In the Major alone was vested the power to impose penance upon and to receive lapsed brethren, but the addition of treachery *ipso facto* precluded any re-admission, for treachery was the unpardonable sin. Penance was imposed in a prescribed form.* The Order of Major also carried with it the duty of preaching and making (*conficere*) the Body and Blood of Christ, and authority to commission Presbyters to do the same, except that at Easter only Majors could consecrate at Holy Communion.†

The heretics regarded their Orders as in no whit inferior to those of the Roman Church. To their own and Roman Bishops alike they denied the powers of the Keys of the Kingdom of Heaven, as then understood, but their powers of absolution were the same, seeing that both had the Apostolic Succession through the Holy Spirit. But this recognition of Roman Orders was only ideal and theoretical, because the heretics maintained that the Roman Church had practically forfeited its authority through its corruptions and persecutions. The Catharists regarded this forfeiture as irremediable and final : the Waldenses as recoverable by repentance and reformation along the lines of their own tenets. In this way we may reconcile the conflict of evidence as to the relationship between Catholic and heretical Orders.

* *v. infra*, p. 86.   † *v. infra*, p. 81.

CHAPTER IV

(continued)

(B) RITES AND CEREMONIES

§ I. THE LORD'S SUPPER

THE Records of the Inquisition of Languedoc* (beginning of the fourteenth century) preserve a description of the Lord's Supper on Good Friday which is uncorroborated. " The Major on the Day of the Supper after the ninth hour, when the Supper has been prepared, washes the feet of the company (*sociorum*). He then places himself with them at the table, and blesses the bread, wine and fish, not as a sacrifice or offering (*holocaustum*), but in memory of the Lord's Supper, and prays as follows : ' O Lord God of Abraham, Isaac and Jacob, God of our fathers, and Father of our Lord Jesus Christ, Who by the hands of the Bishops and Presbyters, Thy servants, hast commanded sacrifices and offerings and various oblations to be offered : O Lord Jesus Christ, Who didst bless the five loaves and two fishes in the wilderness, and blessing water didst turn it into wine : bless in the name of the Father, Son and Holy Spirit this bread, fish and wine, not as a sacrifice or offering, but in simple commemoration of the most holy Supper of Jesus Christ and His disciples, since, O Lord, I do not dare to offer to Thee by impure hands and defiled mouth the sacrifice of our Lord Bishop,

* Cod. Vat. 4030.

Jesus Christ Thy Son, but this bread and the substance of this fish and wine we beseech Thee to bless in the name of the Father, Son and Holy Spirit, and may the communion (*communicatio*) of this bread as a simple Host please Thee, Eternal Father, and so direct my soul and my body, even all my senses, and so guide my footsteps that I may be worthy to offer Thee that most sacred Body which is worshipped by angels in heaven.' ''
The Major eats and drinks first, and then distributes to others.

This, however, did not take the place of the celebration on Easter Day, which was the most important of the whole year, and devolved upon a Major only. For this highest service of the year the Major was the better prepared (*melius dispositus*) by the Lenten Fast, and particularly by the more severe fast upon bread and water only for three days previously. When the congregation, of both sexes, is assembled, a table or bench is spread with a clean cloth, and a cup of good pure wine and a cake or loaf, unleavened, placed upon it. Then the president says : " Let us ask God to forgive us our sins for His mercy's sake, and to fill us with those things which we ask worthily, for His mercy's sake, and let us say seven times the Pater noster to the honour of God and the Holy Trinity." This the congregation does on bended knee. Then the president takes a napkin (*tersorium*) and, hanging it over his left shoulder, with his bare right hand he wraps the loaf (*panis*) or cake (*placenta*) wholly in the napkin and holds it thus to his breast. Standing thus he repeats (some said " inaudibly ") the exact words our Lord used at the Institution.* He then makes the sign over (*signat*) the bread and the wine, breaking (or cutting with a small knife lengthwise) the bread. During these ceremonies the congregation

* *v.* pp. 47, note, 62.

stand, but at this point they and he seat themselves at the table according to (Church) rank. As each receives the bread and wine from him, he (the recipient) says : " Benedicité, Senher," and he replies, " Deus vos benedicat." Thus " their sacrifice is finished, and they believe that this is the Body and Blood of Jesus Christ." The remains, if any, are reserved (*conservari*) until after Easter, when they are consumed by the faithful.

§ 2. GRACE AT MEALS

First of all they stand in silent prayer, long enough to say thirty or forty Pater nosters. Before sitting down they all bless the table by saying, " Benedicite, Kyrie Eleison, Christe Eleison, Kyrie Eleison." Then the eldest says in the vulgar tongue, " God, Who blessed the five loaves and two fishes in the wilderness for His disciples, bless this table and the things that are on it and shall be placed upon it," and he makes the sign of the cross saying : " In the Name of the Father, Son and Holy Spirit." After the meal the Elder gives thanks, saying in the vulgar tongue Revelation vii. 12, adding : " May God give good reward and food to all who benefit and bless us : may God Who gives us temporal food give us spiritual food : may God be with us and we with Him always," and the rest answer, Amen. In blessing the table and in returning thanks they lift their hands clasped and faces to heaven. Then, if time and place were opportune, would follow a sermon or instruction, but this was usually deferred until after supper when the day's work was done, and they could speak with less danger, and, if prudence suggested, in the dark. Teaching was positive rather than negative, for they began not by denouncing the errors and vices of others, but by pointing out what being a disciple of Christ involved according to the Scriptures. These they had in the vulgar tongue, as well as in Latin. They would " read round," and those who could not read would repeat from memory. They further supported their tenets by " saint and doctor."

§ 3. THE CONSOLAMENTUM

This rite was, according to Reinéri Saccho, peculiar to the Catharists, who gave it the alternative title of Imposition of hands, but Catholics, Heretication.* By it Catharists believed that a person received the gift of the Holy Ghost the Consolator, or Comforter—hence its name, and those who submitted to the rites were called Consolati. Hence, as only those were admitted who had proved themselves staunch and true to Catharism, they were called indifferently Consolati or Perfecti, although more strictly, the former was applicable only to the Catharists, and the latter to the Waldenses. Many who shrank from the austere life which the Consolamentum demanded postponed it until what they supposed to be their last illness, so that the ceremonies had to be altered to suit the circumstances, provided always that the imposition of hands was retained. The person to be " consoled " must, if in health, prepare himself by a three days' rigorous fast. At the service of initiation, a table or bench covered with white towels and a book, called the Text, upon it, were placed in the midst of the congregation arranged according to Church rank. Within their midst, but at some distance from the table, stood the candidate. The minister at the head of the table reminded him of the ascetic life he would have to lead, the dangers and persecutions he would have to endure, and that lapse meant eternal damnation, for there was no salvation in the Roman Church. He was then asked

* Also, more rarely, la Convenenza or the Agreement.

if, with all this before him, he would surrender himself wholly to God and the Gospel. On his answering, Yes, he was further asked whether he would promise never to eat meat, eggs, cheese, venison, oil or fish, never to lie or swear, never to indulge any lust, never to touch a woman, never to kill, never to eat without a companion or without saying the Lord's Prayer, never to sleep unclothed, never to betray the Faith. Having made these promises, the candidate advanced towards the minister by certain, usually three, stages (*intervalla*), making at each stage his " melioramentum," i.e. he bent the knee, touching the ground with his hands and saying, " Benedicite," thus shewing that the minister was better (*melior*) than himself.* At each stage the minister replied, " Deus vos benedicat." On reaching the table he said : " Good Christians, I beg for God's blessing and yours. Pray to God that He may keep me from a bad death, and bring me to a good end and to the hands of good Christians." Then the minister gave him the book to kiss, and placed it upon his head. Then all placed their hands upon his head or shoulders, saying : " We worship Thee, Father, Son and Holy Ghost," and the minister prayed that the Holy Ghost the Consolator might descend upon him. When all had said the Lord's Prayer, the minister read St. John i. 1-17. He then gave the candidate the kiss of peace, and the candidate to the one next to him, and so on until all the congregation had exchanged the salutation. If the " consoled " were a woman, the minister, instead, touched her shoulder with the book, and her elbow with his elbow, and she did the same, if the one next to her were a man. He (or she) was given a small cord, " quo pro haeresi cingeretur," to be worn round the body, next to the skin. The con-

---

* This obeisance was made to him not personally but officially, as merely the instrument or agent of the Holy Spirit.

gregation then separated, after congratulating the new member.

In the case of the sick, treatment varied. Some would not " console " anyone not in full possession of his faculties and able to make the answers. Others admitted such, provided that in some way other than by speech he signified his assent. Others went further and " consoled " even the unconscious at the urgent request of his friends anxious for his eternal welfare. Thus sometimes even children were " consoled." In these cases certain modifications were allowed in the ritual. Thus if the sick man could not make his melioramentum, the minister took his hands within his own, and the sick man would say " Benedicite," bending his head each time. If he could not say the Lord's Prayer, others would say it for him. If it were discovered that the officiating minister was in mortal sin (according to Catharist law), the Consolamentum was invalid.

§ 4. THE ENDURA

Every inducement was now made to the sick man to end his life by any means other than by direct violence. He was urged to undergo the *Endura*, which took various forms. We read of this as early as A.D. 1028 in connection with a community at Montfort, near Turin, which taught that death by illness or senile decay only shewed that Satan was still master of the situation and could send the soul into another body. Here probably we have the clue to the reasons for encouraging the practice of the Endura. The " consoled " had solemnly promised not to kill, and therefore could not directly commit suicide. But he could consummate the purpose of God, Who had sent him the illness, by indirect means, and thwart the world, the flesh and the devil by a speedy death.

Several expedients were adopted. Thus the " consoled " sick was asked whether he would be a martyr or a confessor. If he said the former, a cushion or pillow was held over his mouth for some time. Whether he recovered or succumbed, he was henceforth held to be a martyr. If he said, a confessor, he had to remain three days without food and drink, and whether the fast proved fatal or not, he was called a confessor. At Ax, Peter Autéri, after some hesitation, " consoled " an unconscious woman, and ordered that nothing should be given her but pure water. She recovered and asked for food, which, however, her daughter refused on religious grounds, but the mother indignantly declined to be bound by promises made for her by others. Mengard, a woman examined at Carcassonne in A.D. 1308, said her little boy was hereticated when at the point of death, and she was ordered to give him nothing but bread and water, for when he died he would be an angel. But she refused not to give him the breast, and so he was not fully hereticated. At the same Inquisition Raymond Issaun said that his brother, William, after heretication had placed himself completely in the Endura for about seven weeks, and stayed in a certain hut where he died, and he was buried in the house of their father. Another method was opening a vein and slowly bleeding to death in a bath ; another, drinking the juice of wild cucumbers mixed with powdered glass so that the intestines were torn to pieces.

§ 5. PENANCE

This was administered by the Major, or by a Presbyter by delegation in minor offences. After the penitent had confessed, the Major (or Presbyter) pointed out how and to what extent he had offended against the Holy Scriptures, and imposed a penance accordingly, saying : " I, being entrusted with the authority of the blessed Apostles Peter and Paul, bid thee on behalf of our Lord Jesus Christ Who instituted this holy sacrament of penance in His Church, perform such penance as I impose upon thee."* No indulgences were granted. Absolution was from the fault, not from its punishment.

§ 6. FASTS

" The Manichees of modern times," as they are called in the Acts of the Inquisition at Carcassonne, had three Fasts of forty days during the year. (*a*) From St. Britius (Nov. 13th) to Christmas. (*b*) Lent. (*c*) From Whitsun to SS. Peter and Paul (June 29th), which, therefore, could not always have been forty days. The first and last week of each Fast they called " strict," for then they fasted on bread and water, but in the other weeks of the Fast on only three days—Monday, Wednesday and Friday. Others observed these three days as Fasts throughout the year, unless they were travelling or were ill. Others, again, because flesh was repulsive to them, and to mark their difference from the Roman Church, would eat flesh on Roman Fast days, *but not* when their own and Roman Fasts coincided.

* *v. supra*, p. 66.

CHAPTER V

A SUMMARY

IN attempting to summarize the foregoing testimonies of friend and foe we must again guard ourselves against the inference that doctrinal similarity with previous heresies involves organic succession. Historical links fail us when we attempt to construct the genealogical table. The general fact to be recognized is that while the Catholic Church had expelled those ancient heresies from her doors, their odour remained, and, remaining, reminded her members of problems about God and man, spirit and flesh, time and eternity to which only revelation, and not speculation, could supply the answer.

The Nature of God. The resemblance between the Dualism of Gnosticism and Catharism is obvious. Each taught both an absolute and a modified Dualism ; but a closer study shews us that whereas with Gnosticism (and particularly Manicheism) this dogma was fundamental, with Catharism it became more and more subordinate to discipline and conduct. It was offered as a solution to the mystery of evil, but in the catechizing of their candidates for membership, no question touching Dualism was put to them. Thus discipline of life was presented to them not as a struggle with an evil God, but as a following of Apostolic Christianity and a practical protest against a corrupt hierarchy. The Lord's Prayer was used as much as a Creed as a Prayer, yet there is not the slightest evidence that they understood " ἀπὸ τοῦ πονηροῦ " to be " from the evil *one*."

The Nature of Christ. The Albigenses were constantly charged with holding Docetic views of Christ. Yet they believed in an Incarnation, though not that of the Nicene Creed. They were prepared to say that Christ was born " in virgine," but not " ex virgine," or as the Paulicians put it, " δι' αὐτῆς ὡς διὰ σωλῆνος διεληλυθέναι." The basic belief in the utter sinfulness of flesh was an insuperable obstacle to belief in the sinlessness of the Incarnate Christ, an obstacle which late in Christianity the theory of the Immaculate Conception attempts to surmount. The Manichees, under Parsic influence, taught that as " the light shineth in the darkness, and the darkness overcame it not," so the Christ could not enter a human body, except in appearance ; and the Priscillianists denied a human body to Him, and said He was innascibilis, because the human body was the seat of sin. The Albigensian solution was that Christ was created sinless man in heaven, and in His perfect nature of body, soul and spirit was born in the Virgin Mary. The one passage of Scripture which was read at their distinctive service—the Consolamentum—was St. John i. 1–17, where the order is " the Word was made flesh and (then) dwelt among us." The two clauses in the Creed, therefore, should be reversed and run : " He was made man, and came down from heaven." It followed from this real humanity of Christ that His suffering was real and not Docetic. Hence the Albigenses regarded the Cross as an instrument and symbol of the actual shame and suffering of Christ, and, as such, should not be honoured.

The Nature of the Holy Ghost. Although the Albigenses in their services paid worship to the Holy Trinity by their frequent " Adoremus," they did not accept the

position of the Council of Chalcedon. Both the Son and
the Holy Spirit were, according to them, created by God
the Father, and there was a difference of essence (*sub-
stantia*) between the three Persons. The Father was
greater than the Son (St. John xiv. 28) and the Holy
Ghost, and the Son greater than the Holy Ghost. The
Holy Ghost did not function in the world until after the
Ascension of Christ. He does not Himself enter into
man at the imposition of hands. The perfect man as
made in the image of God has a tripartite nature of body,
soul (*anima*) and spirit. Owing to sin man's spirit went
back to heaven, and hence the present imperfect man
consists of corpus and anima. But the spiritus of each
man is guardian and guide (*custos, rector*) of the anima,
and is restored to him by the Paraclete or Principal
(i.e. *the* Holy) Spirit by the imposition of hands.*

The Nature of their Church. The basis of Gnosticism
was knowledge (γνῶσις), but that of Catharism faith
(*fides*). The Gnostics or γνωστικοί repelled the πιστικοί,
whereas the πιστικοί or Credents formed the great
majority of the Catharists. Gnosticism was esoteric,
Catharism exoteric. Gnosticism was intellectual, Catharism spiritual. Catharism taught that none could be
saved outside its fold, but none were predestined from
entering that fold. If this is Gnosticism it is the
Gnosticism of Marcion, the mildest of all Gnostics.
(The only exception to this " Catholicism " was due to
the emphasis which the Catharists laid upon Faith itself,
whereby they were led to exclude infants from member-

---

* This is Moneta's view. Moneta's great work is the chief, as it is
the only contemporary systematic investigation of Catharism. It was
published under the editorship of Augustine Riccheni, Professor at
Bologna, at Rome in A.D. 1743. Of Moneta himself we know little.
He was born at Cremona, and, fired by the eloquence of the Dominican
Friar, Reginald, entered that Order in A.D. 1220, an Order which arose
specially to combat Albigensianism. He was appointed Censor of the
Faith at Milan, and died some time after A.D. 1240.

ship, because they could not be certain of a member's faith until he avowed it.) Hence, where Gnostics founded schools, admission to which was grudgingly granted, Catharism founded churches with an ever-open door for all.

The movement failed—failed in spite of all its zeal, self-sacrifice, sincerity and Scripturalness. With the political and military forces ultimately brought to bear against it we are not here concerned. Without these, however, it was doomed to failure through its own weaknesses and divisions. It was a bold bid for freedom of thought and speech in all matters of religion. It was a revolt against the assumption that all must believe alike, and that the laity must never question what the priesthood taught. The Infallibility of the Church had become practically an Article of the Faith. And because this indefeasible right of man was declared by the Church to be indefensible, independence changed into intolerance, and freedom into disruption. But any upheaval, social or religious, to be successful must be united and progressive. It must be of one heart and one mind in defence and attack. It must also convince the people that it has recovered old truths or discovered new. The indispensable Foundation of Belief is one God : a religion which starts with two, and yet protests that it is Christian, whatever other merits it may possess, can never attract and retain the adherence of that or any other age, whatever relation it might seek to establish between the two. Catharism from the very beginning was a house divided against itself as to the God of its worship and obedience. The Albigensian Christ offered no Atonement, all-sufficient and complete, for the sins of men, and so brought to men no peace which passeth all understanding. Their " perfect " life was impracticable and would have brought society to an end. All agree that the Waldenses, who started *de novo* from the Scriptures, and endeavoured to live and teach according to their precepts, began solely as reformers and not as schismatics. Yet even they could not keep themselves untainted by the stronger and more numerous Catharists, and it was easy for their enemies to convince an uncritical age that there was little difference between them. The Albigenses have perished, the Waldenses remain, and such seekers after truth ever will, who

" Correct the portrait by the living face,
Man's God by God's God, in the mind of man."

INDEX

93